A Chemicals Perspective on Designing with Sustainable Plastics

GOALS, CONSIDERATIONS AND TRADE-OFFS

))OECD

BETTER POLICIES FOR BETTER LIVES

This document, as well as any data and map included herein, are without prejudice to the status of or sovereignty over any territory, to the delimitation of international frontiers and boundaries and to the name of any territory, city or area.

Please cite this publication as:
OECD (2021), *A Chemicals Perspective on Designing with Sustainable Plastics : Goals, Considerations and Trade-offs*, OECD Publishing, Paris, *https://doi.org/10.1787/f2ba8ff3-en*.

ISBN 978-92-64-68375-4 (print)
ISBN 978-92-64-77288-5 (pdf)

Foreword

This study builds upon the general considerations from the OECD report 'Considerations and criteria of sustainable plastics from a chemicals perspective' published in 2018. It also builds on sector specific considerations from four case studies on insulation, flooring, biscuit wrappers, and detergent bottles.

The insights gathered in these reports emanated from literature reviews, interviews and workshops with chemists and suppliers, and were reviewed by OECD country delegates and stakeholders. Experts nominated via the OECD's Chemicals and Biotechnology Committee (CBC) and the Environmental Policy Committee's Working Party on Resource Productivity and Waste (WPRPW) provided valuable input during an online workshop held on the 9th and 10th of March 2021. The workshop was supported by voluntary contributions from Japan and the United Kingdom. The development of this report and the case studies has been supported by voluntary contributions from Japan and Switzerland.

A team of industrial design engineers specialised in design for a circular economy from the company Partners for Innovation consolidated the insights from these reports and the workshop to develop a draft document on which this report is based.

This report was then reviewed by experts nominated by the CBC and WPRPW, followed by a review by the Working Party for Risk Management (WPRM) and the Working Party on Resource Productivity and Waste (WPRPW). It is published under the responsibility of the CBC.

Table of contents

Tables

Figures

Boxes

Follow OECD Publications on:

http://twitter.com/OECD_Pubs

http://www.facebook.com/OECDPublications

http://www.linkedin.com/groups/OECD-Publications-4645871

http://www.youtube.com/oecdilibrary

http://www.oecd.org/oecddirect/

List of Abbreviations

ACS	American Chemical Society
CBC	Chemicals and Biotechnology Committee
CHA	Chemical Hazard Assessment
CMR	Carcinogenic, mutagenic, or toxic to reproduction
DfCE	Design for a Circular Economy
ECHA	European Chemicals Agency
EDC	Endocrine-Disrupting Chemicals
EEE	Electrical and Electronic Equipment
GADSL	Global Automotive Declarable Substance List
GCI	Green Chemistry Institute
HCl	Hydrogen Chloride
LCA	Life Cycle Assessment
NIAS	Non-intentionally added substances
OECD	Organisation for Economic Co-operation and Development
PBT	Persistent, Bioaccumulative and/or Toxic
PMT	Persistent, Mobile, and Toxic
POP	Persistent Organic Pollutants
SIN	Substitute It Now
SVHC	Substance of Very High Concern
VOC	Volatile Organic Compound
vPvB	very Persistent and very Bioaccumulative
WEEE	Waste Electrical and Electronic Equipment
WPRM	Working Party on Risk Management
WPRPW	Working Party on Resource Productivity and Waste

Executive Summary

The development of plastic products does not systematically take sustainability, particularly from a chemicals perspective, into account. The challenge in creating sustainable plastic products revolves around the selection of sustainable materials, but also the overall system within which the product circulates. A sustainable plastic product operates in a system, to which the design of the product and its plastic materials are adapted.

The objective of this document is to enable the creation of inherently sustainable plastic products by integrating sustainable chemistry thinking in the design process. Sustainable plastics have been outlined by the OECD to be "plastics used in products that provide societal benefits while enhancing human and environmental health and safety across the entire product life cycle".

This study builds on the OECD report 'Considerations and criteria of sustainable plastics from a chemicals perspective' and four OECD case studies in the building and packaging sectors.

The report focuses on the chemicals perspective of the material selection process when plastic is the material of choice. While other material choices could provide sustainable solutions and should be considered at the design stage, this is not within the scope of the report. The information presented equips designers and engineers with knowledge of how to manage the complexity of finding the most sustainable plastic for their products. The main contributions of this report are an overall approach to sustainable plastic selection from a chemicals perspective, and the identification of a set of generalizable sustainable design goals, life cycle considerations and trade-offs. While other elements also factor into selection of a sustainable solution (e.g. economic, societal), these are not within the scope of this report.

Designers need to set sustainable design goals as they consider sustainable plastics selection from a chemicals perspective. It is recommended that these build upon the following set of principles derived from the American Chemical Society (ACS) Green Chemistry Institute's (GC) design principles of sustainable chemistry and engineering:

- Maximise resource efficiency.
- Eliminate and minimise hazards and pollution.
- Design systems holistically and using life cycle thinking.

Based on the principles, the following sustainable design goals can be set and also added to depending on the level of ambition of the company. These design goals are further elaborated in the report.

- Select materials with an inherently low risk/hazard.
- Select materials that have a commercial 'afterlife'.
- Select materials that generate no waste.
- Select materials that use secondary feedstock or biobased feedstock.

At a final, more granular level, the following general considerations for sustainable design from a chemicals perspective were identified as key elements for designers to take into account for each life-cycle phase when selecting material composition. While presented as the main considerations of individual phases, ultimately these considerations are brought together as a whole-product assessment and optimisation taking the whole life-cycle into account.

Considerations during the sourcing phase

A. Select a base polymer (secondary or primary renewable source; secondary or primary non-renewable source) that:
- the least emissions during extraction and production.
- uses non-hazardous or the least hazardous chemicals during extraction and production.
- minimises worker exposure during extraction and production.

B. Primary renewable feedstock (i.e., bio(based)plastics) is potentially a sustainable source, when:
- the benefits of using this feedstock, demonstrated through life-cycle assessment, outweigh the costs of externalities, such as water consumption, and competition with food production or social or ecological land use.
- the availability and continuity of availability of the supply of the feedstock enables its use.

C. Secondary feedstock is potentially a sustainable source, when
- the propagation of hazardous chemicals is avoided.
- the resulting material contains a high percentage of the recycled material when designed.
- the current and future availability of the supply of the secondary feedstock enables its use.

D. Primary non-renewable feedstock can be used as last resort, if it minimises hazardous chemicals or hazardous mixtures of chemicals.

E. Strive for transparency in chemical compositions throughout the value chain.

Considerations during the manufacturing phase

A. Select a manufacturing technique that:
- generates the least emissions.
- uses the least processing aids.
- uses non-hazardous or the least hazardous chemicals.
- minimises worker exposure.

B. Consider sustainable manufacturing on a systems level.

C. Ensure transparency in chemical composition throughout the value chain.

Considerations during the use phase

A. Consider whether the determined chemical and mechanical requirements are strict, or there is flexibility to allow for more sustainable choices.

B. Select a base polymer/source material that:
- generates the least emissions.

- prevents or minimises exposure to hazardous chemicals during use and maintenance.
- enables the intended lifespan of the product.

   C. Map exposure scenarios during use and reduce exposure to hazard as much as possible.

Considerations during the end-of-use phase

A. Minimise the amount of waste at end-of-use through polymer selection.

B. Simplify designs to include as few different polymers as possible.

C. Maximise the production of high-quality recycled materials as output of the recycling process.

D. Minimise the amount of and exposure to chemical hazard at end-of-use through chemical selection.

E. Match the polymer selection to the waste management operations in the intended market.

F. Consider ways to mitigate the risk of littering.

G. Ensure transparency of chemical composition.

These considerations will also lead to trade-offs that will need to be carefully balanced in the decision-making process by the design team, but they are expected to promote transparency and reflection on the implications of making these choices. Ultimately, the report should help to equip designers and engineers with knowledge of relevant chemical considerations when selecting sustainable plastic and support better outcomes as a result.

Chapter 1. Sustainable Design of Plastics: Problem Formulation, Objectives and Scope

This chapter outlines the problem formulation regarding design of sustainable plastics from a chemicals perspective and provides an overview of the objectives, scope and outline of the document.

1.1. Rationale

1.1.1. The problem

Annual global plastics production reached 430 million metric tons in 2019 and could continue to grow to 1,150 million metric tons in 2060 (OECD, forthcoming). While plastics deliver many benefits to society, the chemical components of plastics can have negative impacts on human health and the environment. Potential chemical hazards can arise in all lifecycle phases from sourcing until end-of-life. More than 10 000 chemicals including monomers, additives and processing aides have been identified to be used in plastics, with almost one quarter of them of potential concern (Wiesinger et al., 2021).

The development of plastic products currently does not always take sustainability into account. As defined by the OECD, **sustainable plastics** are "plastics used in products that provide societal benefits while enhancing human and environmental health and safety across the entire product life cycle" (OECD, 2018a). Sustainable plastics should limit the creation of waste, toxins and pollution from their inception to their next use or end-of-life. They should thus have a reduced (negative) impact on the climate, help promote a more circular economy and help meet the objectives of the United Nations Sustainable Development Goals.

The challenge in creating sustainable plastic products revolves around the selection of sustainable materials, but also the overall system within which the product circulates. As visualised in Figure 1.1, when studying sustainable plastics, the system, product, materials and chemical aspects are interrelated. A sustainable plastic product operates in a system, to which the design of the product and its plastic materials are adapted. For example, at the end-of-life, the product should be able to be collected, the plastics sorted and recycled in the facilities that are operational at the time of disposal in that geographical area.

Figure 1.1. Relationship between system, product, materials and a chemicals perspective. The chemicals perspective is interconnected with design decisions made at a system, product and material level.

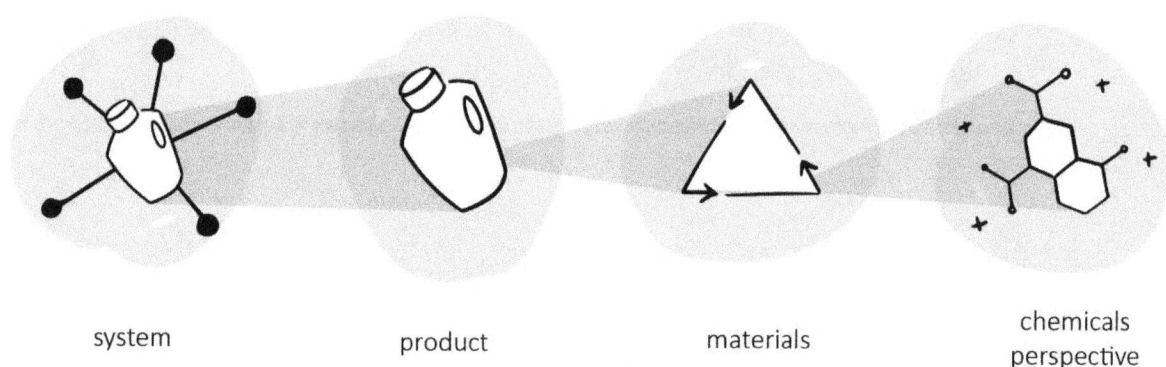

| system | product | materials | chemicals perspective |

In a circular economy, the system is restorative by design and keeps the value and utility of products, components, and materials at their highest level over time (Webster, 2015). The body of work on designing for a circular economy provides guidance to designers and engineers at a system and product design level (see Box 1.1).

Box 1.1. Design for a Circular Economy (DfCE)

In a circular economy, products and components are designed to be kept at their highest utility and value at all times, and the system around them is regenerative by design (Ellen MacArthur Foundation, 2013). As illustrated on the right in Figure 1.2, the product is designed to be preferably repaired, reused, then refurbished and remanufactured, and if little value remains, finally recycled. The mining of virgin materials and leakages (i.e., energy recovery and landfill) are to be minimised. Biological nutrients, represented on the left-hand side of Figure 1.2, are resources that can return to the biosphere to biodegrade after their use.

The basics of circular economy

DfCE is guided by the following main principles (Ellen MacArthur Foundation, 2013):

- Design out waste by designing systems and products using resources that will never be lost
- Distinguish biological and technological nutrients to find the most appropriate solutions for consumables and durable products
- Use renewable energy

Design and business strategies

Various design strategies can be implemented to enable a transition towards a circular economy. These, for instance, include designing for long-life products, design for product-life extension, and design for dis- and reassembly (Moreno, De los Rios, Rowe, and Charnley, 2016).

Business model strategies are also of essence in a circular economy. Different design interventions are needed depending on whether the product is accessed by the user through an access or performance model versus in a classic long life (Bocken, de Pauw, and Bakker, 2016).

DfCE methods and tools

DfCE methods and tools are summarised amongst others in the Circular Design Guide developed by IDEO and the Ellen MacArthur Foundation (IDEO and Ellen MacArthur Foundation, 2017), and the Massive Open Online Course 'Circular Economy: An Introduction' by Delft University of Technology (TU Delft, 2021).

Figure 1.2. The Circular Economy according to the Ellen MacArthur Foundation

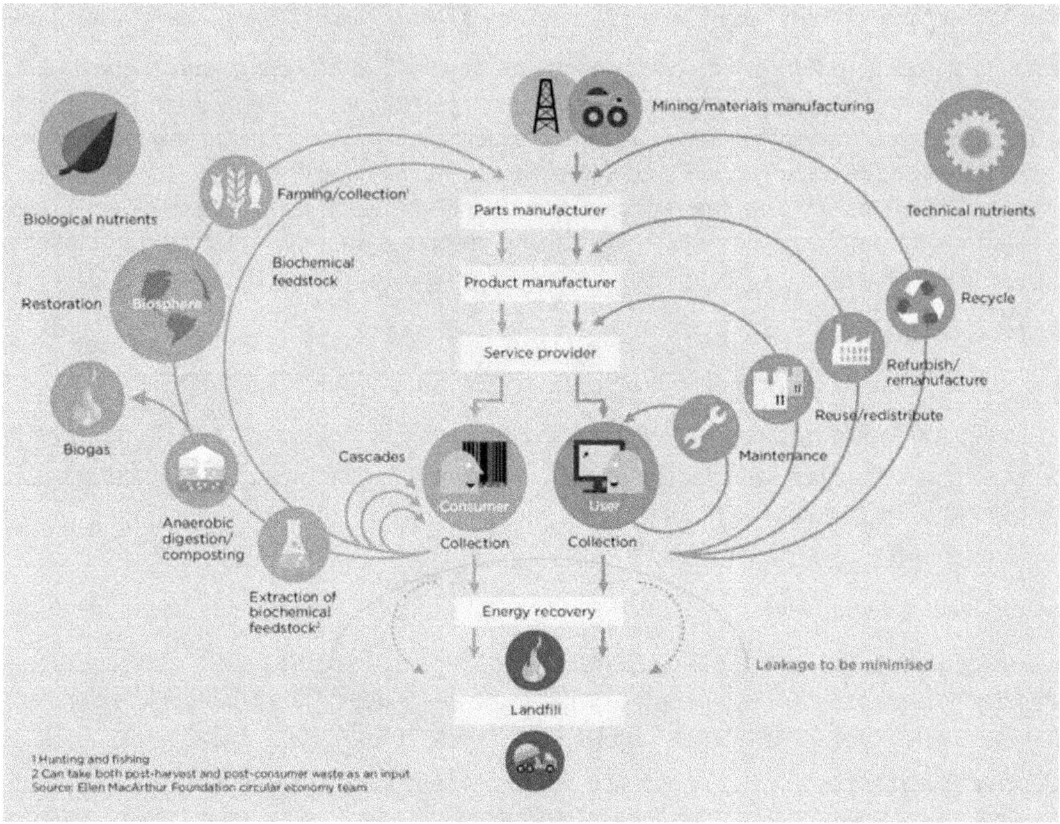

Source: Copyright © Ellen MacArthur Foundation, Towards the circular economy Volume 1: Economic and business rationale for an accelerated transition (2013).

At the foundational level of Figure 1.1, the chemicals perspective encompasses various aspects:

- **Polymer class**: classification of polymers based on properties (e.g. thermoplastics or thermosets)
- **Polymer type**: a specific sort of polymer within a polymer class (e.g. PET or PP)
- **Grade**: a specific structure and molecular mass within a polymer type
- **Additives**: substances added to the polymer to improve its properties (e.g. pigment or flame retardant)
- **Blends**: combination of polymers (e.g. thermoplastic-thermoplastic blend)
- **Production residues**: substances that do not deliberately remain in the material (e.g. catalyst or monomer)
- **Non-intentionally added substances (NIAS)**: substances that have not been deliberately added to the material or unplanned new substances resulting from contact to other materials (e.g. due to degradation substances that leach into the material)

Unfortunately, the knowledge required to develop sustainable plastics from a chemicals perspective may not be well known to designers and engineers who do not have specialised knowledge of chemistry. Ideally, a design team should work closely with chemical sustainability experts to navigate the design process in order to create sustainable plastic products while considering a chemicals perspective.

1.1.2. Chemicals perspective on sustainable plastic

To guide in the creation of sustainable plastic products, a sustainable chemical perspective can be adopted. **Sustainable chemistry** seeks to improve the efficiency, effectiveness, safety and environmental impact of chemical substances and processes (OECD, n.d.).

The sustainable design goals and considerations discussed in this report and the source reports (OECD, 2018a; OECD, 2021a; OECD, 2021b; OECD, 2021c; OECD, 2021d) build upon the American Chemical Society (ACS) Green Chemistry Institute's (GCI) design principles for sustainable chemistry and engineering (American Chemical Society Green Chemistry Institute, 2015). These design principles were based on inter alia Anastas and Warner (1998) and Abraham and Nguyen (2003).

The ACS GCI's design principles were clustered in three categories and need to be applied simultaneously (OECD, 2018a):

- **Maximise resource efficiency**. Resource efficiency means doing more with less while preserving natural capital. Renewable resources should be used at a pace enabling regeneration. Non-renewable resources should be kept in the loop, as waste is the result of system inefficiency.

- **Eliminate and minimise hazards and pollution**. By reducing the hazards of chemicals and the human and environmental exposure to these hazards, the negative impact of plastics on human health and the environment decreases. This, for instance, includes direct effects of plastic chemicals on human health and other species as well as indirect effects of plastic pollution from littering, which exposes wildlife to waste and in turn likely cause toxic effects as well as enters food chains.

- **Design systems holistically and using life cycle thinking**. As visualised in Figure 1.1, sustainable plastic does not exist in isolation but is rather interrelated to the product and system around it. Also, all the stages in the life cycle of the product have to be studied for the selection of the most sustainable plastic.

In response to the United Nations Environment Assembly (UNEA) Resolution 4/8, UNEP developed a Green and Sustainable Chemistry Framework Manual (United Nations Environment Programme, 2020). It presents ten objectives and guiding considerations for what green and sustainable chemistry seeks to achieve, namely:

1. minimising chemical hazards;
2. avoiding regrettable substitutions and alternatives;
3. sustainable sourcing of resources and feedstocks;
4. advancing sustainability of production processes;
5. advancing sustainability of products;
6. minimising chemical releases and pollution;
7. enabling non-toxic circularity;
8. maximising social benefits;
9. protecting workers, consumers and vulnerable populations; and,
10. developing solutions for sustainability challenges.

Green and sustainable chemistry is an active field. Reports with new insights are published at a rapid pace. Technology to assess and identify hazards or NIAS is being developed. These, in turn, are influenced by the evolution of regulatory frameworks and by technological challenges in assessing toxicity. There are also still many uncertainties and blind spots. When available, product composition inventories are limited by current knowledge as especially not all additives and NIAS are listed. Designers are trained to deal with many uncertainties, but they should be aware of what is certain and what is uncertain in order to make the best decisions.

1.1.3. Background of this report

In 2018, the OECD organised a Global Forum on Environment focused on "Plastics in a Circular Economy: Design of Sustainable Plastics from a Chemicals Perspective". The Forum aimed to incentivise a shift in sustainable chemistry thinking during product design by identifying good practices and a policy framework to reduce the environmental and health impacts of plastics.

The Global Forum included a background paper on the sustainability of plastics from a chemical perspective: 'Background Paper 1 - Considerations and Criteria for Sustainable Plastics from a Chemical Perspective' (OECD, 2018a). The Global Forum concluded that additional OECD work could be done to develop criteria and guidance for sustainable plastics. To differentiate potential sustainability criteria across product categories, four case studies were conducted from the packaging and construction sectors (OECD, 2021a; OECD, 2021b; OECD, 2021c; OECD, 2021d). The general considerations from the background paper form the basis of this report. The case studies were used to deepen the insights from the background paper with practical implications for designers.

1.2. Objective

The objective of this report is to enable the creation of inherently sustainable plastic products by integrating sustainable chemistry thinking in the design process.

This report thus puts sustainable chemistry thinking at the core of the material selection process and provides guidance in how to manage the complexity of sustainable design goals, considerations, and trade-offs. After considering the elements of this report, design teams will be well equipped to select sustainable plastic for their designs and will have increased their awareness on key environmental and health elements.

1.3. Scope

The sustainable design goals, life cycle considerations and trade-offs emanating from this study focus on the sustainable chemical perspective. They support designers and engineers in navigating the uncertainties in the world of chemicals, and the ongoing evolution of chemistry discovery, polymer and product technologies in the world of chemicals. This report does not provide a universal solution to developing sustainable plastics, as designing is not a one-size-fits-all activity. Designing is an iterative process with progressive insights gained over time feeding and altering previous steps. It is also highly dependent on the product, market, systems, the team, and the company, to name but a few factors. Economic factors, which are also key to sustainable solutions, are not within the scope of the report. However, this report gives the necessary knowledge at specific moments of the design process to deal with chemical questions when aiming for the use of sustainable plastic. These sustainable design goals, life cycle considerations and trade-offs inform the material selection on the efficiency, effectiveness, safety on human health and environmental impact of chemical substances and processes.

The study concentrates on the material selection after choosing one product concept and selecting plastic as the optimal material family with which to manufacture a specific part. The first stages in the design process (i.e., need definition and design requirement formulation) are thus out of scope. Nevertheless, as considerable impact can be spared at these stages, it is assumed that a DfCE approach was adopted (see Box 1.1). Material selection goes hand in hand with the manufacturing process, the function of the envisioned product and its shape (Ashby, 2005). This report therefore also mentions repercussions of certain chemical decisions on system, product and material design choices. This positioning in the design process is elaborated further in Chapter 2 on Methodology.

The target audience of this study is broad but primarily focuses on designers and engineers. Nevertheless, designers and engineers do not always have the power and room for these improvements. Therefore, decision makers writing the design briefs and policymakers are also seen as a secondary target audience. The report may also be informative to scientists, including material scientists, chemists, chemical engineers and anyone conducting risk or hazard assessment. System changes will also have to be stimulated by policy makers to bring competitors to collaborate with each other to gain scale and reach the mentioned sustainable design goals. Consequently, although it is assumed that the designers and engineers already have acquired the design/engineering basics, this report gives an overview of these basics to inform policy makers.

The study is not limited to a specific type of plastic or product, nor does it focus on a particular geographical region.

1.4. Outline of this report

This report starts with methodological aspects regarding positioning of material selection in the design process and summarising the key material selection steps for designers and engineers (Chapter 2). Sustainable design goals with respect to chemistry are then clarified (Chapter 3). To achieve these goals, the following chapters dive into the considerations for each stage of the lifecycle, namely sourcing (Chapter 4), manufacturing (Chapter 5), use (Chapter 6) and end-of-use (Chapter 7). The report subsequently zooms out to assess the whole product and explores how the material selection can be optimised for the sustainable design goals (Chapter 8). The report finally summarises the main findings and recommends next steps (Chapter 9).

References

Abraham, M. A. and N. Nguyen (2003), "Green Engineering: Defining the Principles. San Destin Conference", *Environmental Progress*, Vol. 22, No.4, pp. 233-236.

American Chemical Society Green Chemistry Institute (2015), *Design Principles for Sustainable Green Chemistry and Engineering*, https://www.acs.org/content/dam/acsorg/greenchemistry/resources/2015-gci-design-principles.pdf.

Anastas, P. T. and J.C. Warner (1998), *Green Chemistry: Theory and Practice*, Oxford University Press, New York.

Ashby, M. F. (2005), *Materials Selection in Mechanical Design*, 3rd Edition, Elsevier.

Bocken, N. et al. (2016), "Product design and business model strategies for a circular economy", *Journal of Industrial and Production Engineering*, Vol. 22, No.5, pp. 308-320.

Ellen MacArthur Foundation (2013), *Towards the circular economy. Volume 1: Economic and business rationale for an accelerated transition*, United Kingdom, https://ellenmacarthurfoundation.org/towards-the-circular-economy-vol-1-an-economic-and-business-rationale-for-an

IDEO and Ellen MacArthur Foundation (2017), *Circular Design Guide*, Ellen MacArthur Foundation, United Kingdom, https://www.circulardesignguide.com/

Moreno, M. et al. (2016), "A conceptual framework for circular design", *Sustainability*, Vol. 8, No. 9, pp. 937.

OECD (n.d.). "A Definition of Sustainable Chemistry". Retrieved from OECD, Paris. http://www.oecd.org/chemicalsafety/risk-management/sustainablechemistry.htm#:~:text=A%20Definition%20of%20Sustainable%20Chemistry&text=Sustainable%20chemistry%20encompasses%20the%20design,benign%20chemical%20products%20and%20processes.%22

OECD (2018a), "Considerations and criteria for sustainable plastics from a chemicals perspective: Background paper 1. OECD Global Forum on Environment: Plastics in a Circular Economy", *Series on Risk Management*, No. 51, OECD, Paris, https://www.oecd.org/chemicalsafety/risk-management/considerations-and-criteria-for-sustainable-plastics-from-a-chemicals-perspective.pdf

OECD (2021a), "Case Study on Flooring; An example of chemical considerations for sustainable plastics design", *Series on Risk Management*, No. 65, OECD, Paris.

OECD (2021b), "Case Study on Insulation: An example of chemical considerations for sustainable plastics design", *Series on Risk Management*, No.66, OECD, Paris.

OECD (2021c), "Case Study on Detergent Bottles; An example of weighing sustainability criteria for rigid plastic non-food packaging", *Series on Risk Management*, No. 63, OECD, Paris.

OECD (2021d), "Case Study on Biscuit Wrappers; An example of weighing sustainability criteria for plastic flexible food packaging from a chemicals perspective", *Series on Risk Management*, No. 64, OECD, Paris.

TU Delft (2021), *Circular Economy: An introduction*, Online course from Delft University of Technology, Netherlands, https://online-learning.tudelft.nl/courses/circular-economy-design-and-technology/

United Nations Environment Programme (2020), *Green and sustainable chemistry: Framework manual*, Geneva, Switzerland, https://wedocs.unep.org/handle/20.500.11822/34338;jsessionid=90C235C3E0B2E94827A3336BC3EA8E93

Webster, K. (2015), *The Circular Economy - A Wealth of Flows*, Ellen MacArthur Foundation, United Kingdom, https://ellenmacarthurfoundation.org/the-circular-economy-a-wealth-of-flows-2nd-edition

Wiesinger, H. et al. (2021), "Deep Dive into Plastic Monomers, Additives, and Processing Aids", *Environmental Science and Technology* Vol. 55, No.13, pp. 9339-9351

Chapter 2. Methodology

This chapter describes the design process and how material selection is connected to the design process. It also outlines the key aspects that guide designers to ensure integration of sustainable chemistry thinking at the design stage resulting in the general steps of sustainable plastic selection.

2.1. Positioning of Material Selection in the Design Process

This study provides guidance to designers and engineers during the material selection across the design process. Through this design process, an individual or team transposes a need into a solution to this need. Note that, in this report, the design solutions are tangible products (vs services) that will require material selection. As shown in Figure 2.1, the material selection occurs at several levels throughout stages of the design process.

Figure 2.1. Design process stages and material selection

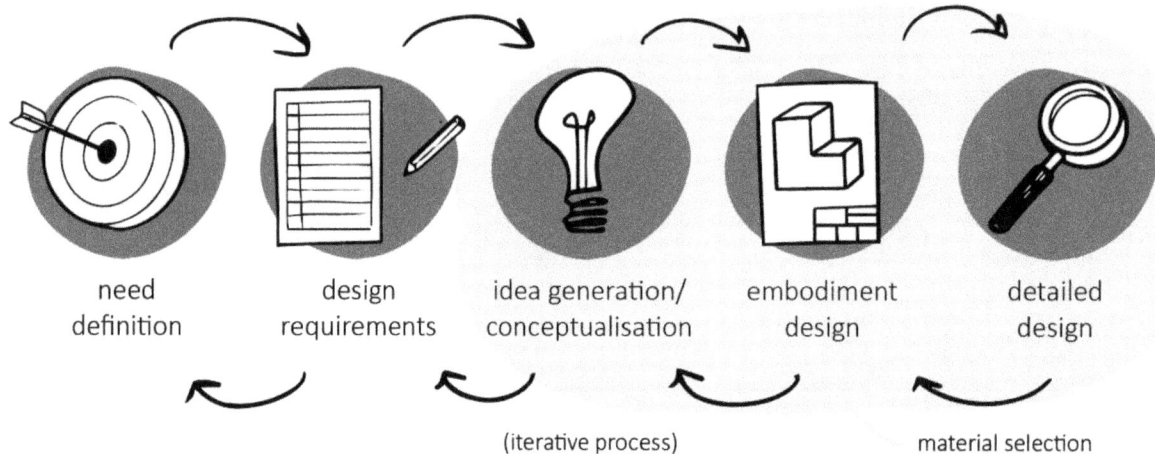

Note: The position of material selection is highlighted in light blue.
Source: Based on Ashby (2005)

The design process is iterative and does not occur linearly. Indeed, the material selection and product design are interconnected. In other words, the material choice influences the design and the design influences the material choice (Ashby, 2005). More specifically, material selection is interconnected with the function of the product/component, its shape, and the production process of the material (Ashby, 2005). For the sake of clarity however, the steps of the material selection are defined in a linear manner.

The starting point of this report is preceded by the need definition stage, the design requirements stage, and the idea generation and conceptualisation stage. These stages occur in consultation with the user or customer.

- **Need definition**: The need for which a solution is being designed was recognised and a product application was identified.

- **Design requirements**: A set of design specifications concerning technical, economic and stakeholder aspects are defined based on the problem analysis. Requirements include for instance performance, target product costs, size and aesthetics. These design requirements are categorised into non-negotiable conditions to be met by the designed product or negotiable conditions that are deemed desirable but are not required.

- **Idea Generation/Conceptualisation**: Product design ideas and concepts were proposed. The concepts were evaluated and one concept was selected as it best fulfilled the design requirements. At this stage, the working principles and function structures of the product are thus determined. Here, needs for material data concern materials overall and require a low level of precision and detail. Plastic was selected as material subset for a specific part of the product.

It is assumed that designers and engineers adopted a Design for a Circular Economy (DfCE) approach during these stages. See Box 1.1 for more information on DfCE.

The material selection in this report starts with plastics and is refined during the embodiment and detailing stages.

- **Embodiment design**: the concept is further developed. More precise and detailed material data is needed to narrow down the selection of the subset of materials (i.e., in this report's case: plastics).
- **Detailed design**: The embodiment design is further developed and results into final product specifications that will enable the production of the product. The highest level of precision and detail of the material data is necessary to make the final choice of a particular material and production process.

2.2. Approaching Sustainable Plastic Selection

As illustrated in Figure 2.2, material selection narrows from the large variety of materials available to designers and engineers, to the specific choice of the material for the to-be-designed product/component. This report focuses on material selection once the material family of polymers was selected for (a part of) the product after a concept was chosen.

Figure 2.2. The general material selection process when choosing a sustainable plastic.

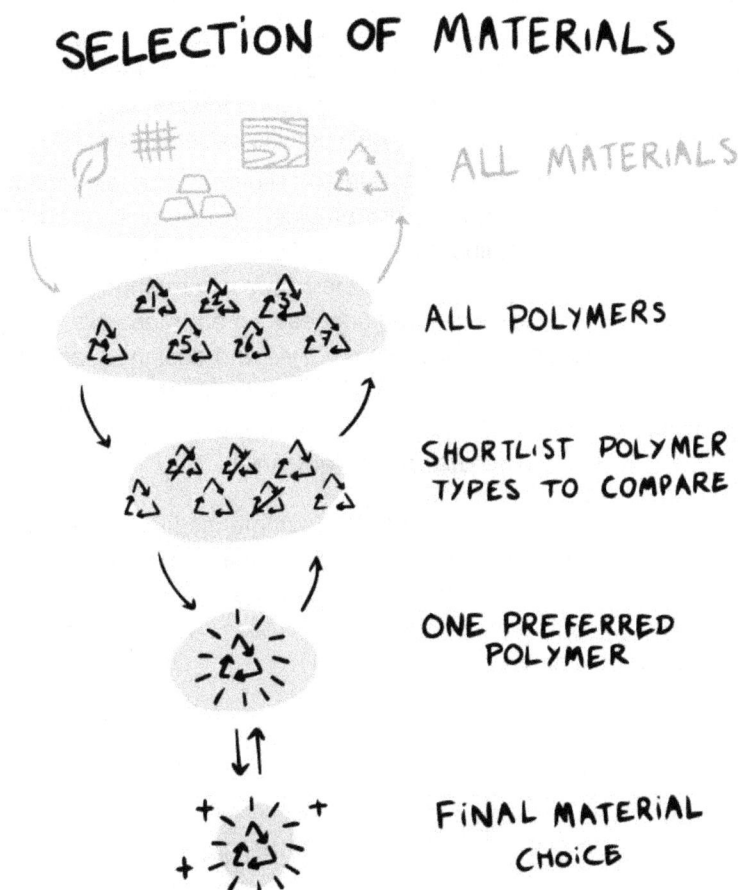

Note: The emphasised steps of the process are the focus of this report, namely the sustainable plastic selection

2.2.1. Levels of guidance during the sustainable plastic selection

Designers and engineers are guided by the following key aspects to integrate chemical thinking during the sustainable plastic selection:

- Design requirements are the non-negotiable conditions to be met by the designed product (i.e., needs) and negotiable conditions that are deemed desirable (i.e., wants). These design requirements include general properties, mechanical, electrical, optical and environmental resistance properties. These are further sharpened based on the product concept selected. They have already been defined by the designers and engineers in the second and third stage of the design process as described above.

- Sustainable design principles are the American Chemical Society (ACS) Green Chemistry Institute's (GCI) design principles of sustainable chemistry and engineering listed in Chapter 1. All these design principles are applied simultaneously.

- Sustainable design goals are derived from the sustainable design principles and provide a more concrete direction for the product design at hand. These have been consolidated from the OECD report on general considerations for sustainable plastic from a chemicals perspective (OECD, 2018a) and the four OECD case studies. They can be found in Chapter 3.

- Chemistry-related sustainability considerations are practical chemical and sustainability matters to be taken into account throughout the life cycle of the to-be-designed product. They go deeper than the sustainability product design goals. These considerations have been consolidated from the five previously mentioned OECD reports. They can be found in Chapters 4-7.

- Trade-offs occur when conflicting aspects need to be balanced during the material selection. The designers and engineers will need to transparently determine how these trade-offs will be resolved at the start of the material selection. These trade-offs have been consolidated from the five previously mentioned OECD reports. They can be found in Chapters 4-7 for trade-offs within life cycle stages and in Chapter 8 for trade-offs between life cycle stages.

- Methods, tools and metrics are chemistry-related resources that designers and engineers can employ to come to decisions. Examples are provided in Annex A and in Technical Tools and Approaches in the Design of Sustainable Plastics (OECD 2018b). Guidance on the use of these tools is not within the scope of this report. As the necessary methods, tools, and metrics depend on the context of the product design, several suggestions are made per category (e.g. measuring circularity and Chemical Hazard Assessment or CHA) and designers and engineers can choose what to use.

2.2.2. Steps of the sustainable plastic selection

The general steps of the sustainable plastic selection are summarised in Figure 2.3. These are based on Ashby (2005), the steps of sustainable plastic selection and continual improvement (OECD, 2018a) and the case studies (OECD, 2021a; OECD, 2021b; OECD, 2021c; OECD, 2021d). The sustainable chemical perspective is integrated throughout the material selection process systematically. Note that the process is iterative and enables continual improvement.

Figure 2.3. Steps of Sustainable Plastics Selection

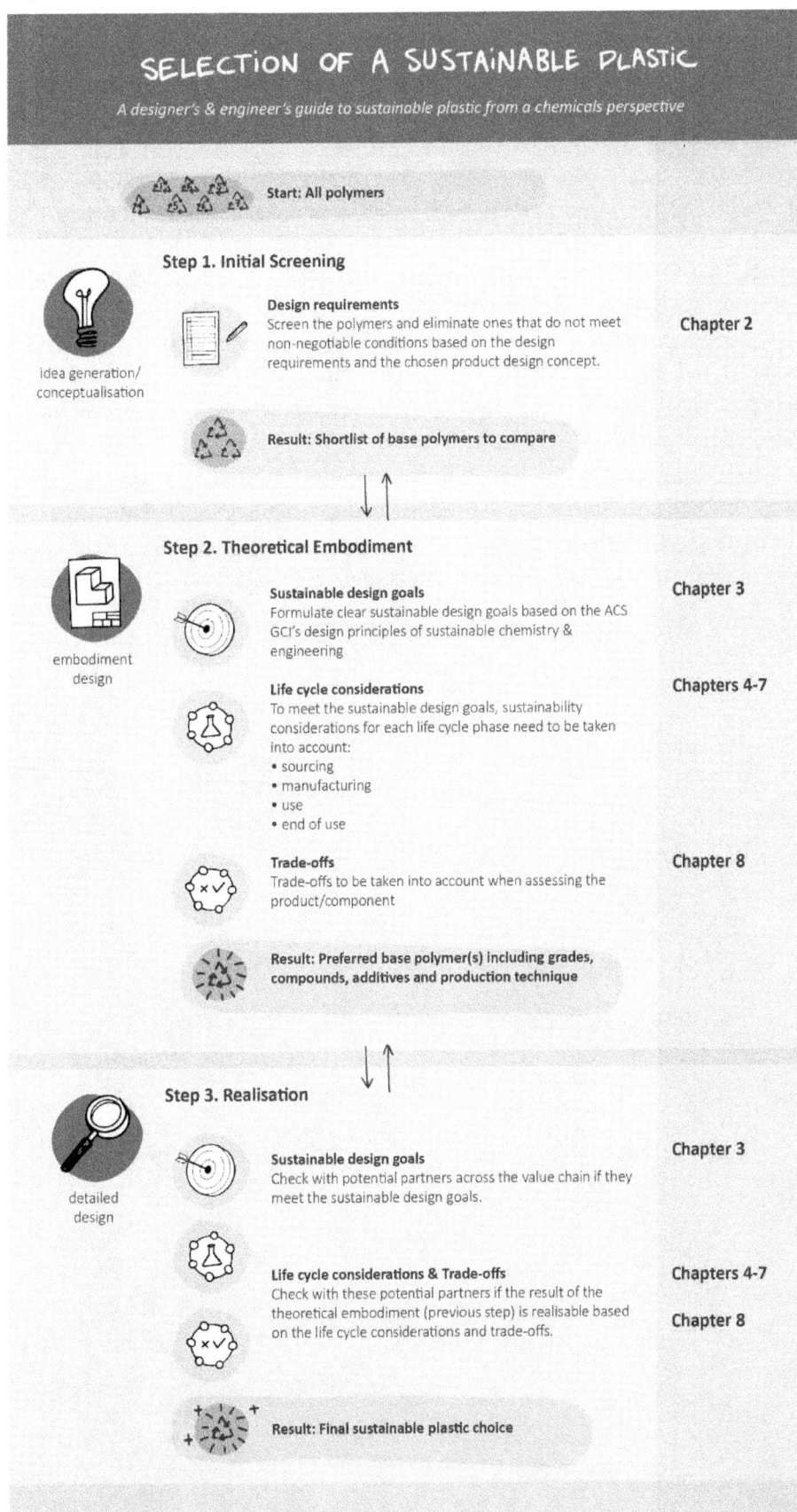

SELECTION OF A SUSTAINABLE PLASTIC
A designer's & engineer's guide to sustainable plastic from a chemicals perspective

Start: All polymers

idea generation/ conceptualisation

Step 1. Initial Screening

Design requirements
Screen the polymers and eliminate ones that do not meet non-negotiable conditions based on the design requirements and the chosen product design concept.

Chapter 2

Result: Shortlist of base polymers to compare

embodiment design

Step 2. Theoretical Embodiment

Sustainable design goals
Formulate clear sustainable design goals based on the ACS GCI's design principles of sustainable chemistry & engineering

Chapter 3

Life cycle considerations
To meet the sustainable design goals, sustainability considerations for each life cycle phase need to be taken into account:
• sourcing
• manufacturing
• use
• end of use

Chapters 4-7

Trade-offs
Trade-offs to be taken into account when assessing the product/component

Chapter 8

Result: Preferred base polymer(s) including grades, compounds, additives and production technique

detailed design

Step 3. Realisation

Sustainable design goals
Check with potential partners across the value chain if they meet the sustainable design goals.

Chapter 3

Life cycle considerations & Trade-offs
Check with these potential partners if the result of the theoretical embodiment (previous step) is realisable based on the life cycle considerations and trade-offs.

Chapters 4-7

Chapter 8

Result: Final sustainable plastic choice

References

Ashby, M. F. (2005), *Materials Selection in Mechanical Design*, 3rd Edition, Elsevier.

OECD (2018a), "Considerations and criteria for sustainable plastics from a chemicals perspective: Background paper 1. OECD Global Forum on Environment: Plastics in a Circular Economy", *Series on Risk Management*, No. 51, OECD, Paris, https://www.oecd.org/chemicalsafety/risk-management/considerations-and-criteria-for-sustainable-plastics-from-a-chemicals-perspective.pdf

OECD (2018b), "Technical Tools and Approaches in the Design of Sustainable Plastics: Background paper 2. OECD Global Forum on Environment: Plastics in a Circular Economy", *Series on Risk Management*, No. 52, OECD, Paris, https://www.oecd.org/chemicalsafety/risk-management/technical-tools-and-approaches-in-the-design-of-sustainable-plastics.pdf

OECD (2021a), "Case Study on Flooring; An example of chemical considerations for sustainable plastics design", *Series on Risk Management*, No. 65, OECD, Paris.

OECD (2021b), "Case Study on Insulation: An example of chemical considerations for sustainable plastics design", *Series on Risk Management*, No.66, OECD, Paris.

OECD (2021c), "Case Study on Detergent Bottles; An example of weighing sustainability criteria for rigid plastic non-food packaging", *Series on Risk Management*, No. 63, OECD, Paris.

OECD (2021d), "Case Study on Biscuit Wrappers; An example of weighing sustainability criteria for plastic flexible food packaging from a chemicals perspective", *Series on Risk Management*, No. 64, OECD, Paris.

Chapter 3. Sustainable Design Goals

This chapter presents the sustainable design goals that should guide sustainable plastics design and also the factors that influence their definition and implementation. Minimally recommended sustainable design goals are describe and mechanisms to consider trade-offs are presented.

A design team will need to set sustainable design goals to guide the sustainable plastic material selection. This chapter first provides examples of sustainable design goals. It then moves to factors influencing the definition of the goals. Finally, this chapter shows how to prepare for future trade-offs emerging from the life cycle considerations.

Note that the process of defining sustainable design goals has to be transparent. The team should report who is responsible for setting the goals, how that is to be done and their minimum requirements.

3.1. Examples of Sustainable Design Goals

Sustainable design goals were formulated in the OECD background paper and the four sectoral case studies to guide material selection, based on the American Chemical Society (ACS) Green Chemistry Institute's (GCI) design principles of sustainable chemistry and engineering.

Sustainable plastics are "plastics used in products that provide societal benefits while enhancing human and environmental health and safety across the entire product life cycle" (OECD, 2018a). As previously visualised in Figure 1.1, the chemicals perspective has repercussions on the material selection, as well as on the product and system design.

3.1.1. The following sustainable design goals are generally relevant:

Select materials with an inherently low risk/hazard

- Hazardous chemicals, especially those with potential for exposure to workers, community, users, and environmental receptors, are eliminated at all life cycle phases or hazardous chemical content is mitigated to levels that do not present risks, including:
  - Base polymer and source materials manufacturing.
  - Product manufacturing, including the life cycles of additives, production residues and non-intentionally added substances (NIAS).
  - During installation and use, including new material combinations (e.g. glue while installing) and interactions with the product (e.g. skin contact).
  - End-of-use (i.e., when the current user ends the product use cycle, independent of the remaining value and utility of the product) including unplanned routes (e.g. littering).

  Designers may adopt a least hazardous approach to chemical selection as a precautionary measure. This will protect against unintentional exposure to hazardous chemicals during circular processing of waste products.

- Transparency in terms of content, hazard properties, emissions and data gaps are necessary at every step of the supply chain. Ideally, full hazard assessments for chemicals present in the finished plastics (and for the possible mixture of migrating chemicals from the plastic) are available.

Select materials that have a commercial 'afterlife'

- Products, services and systems are designed for circular processing at the end-of-use (i.e., reuse, refurbishment, remanufacturing and/or recycling).
- Content transparency and traceability exists to support circular processing.
- Corresponding infrastructure exists to support circular processing.
- Materials are able to undergo multiple cycles of recycling.

Select materials that generate no waste

- Manufacturing waste and waste generated during product installation is avoided at every step of the production process. If this is unavoidable, it should be recycled.
- The plastic product's end-of-use is known and accounted for during material selection so as to avoid the generation of waste.

Select materials that use secondary feedstock or biobased feedstock

- Use biobased/rapidly renewable resources that do not compete with "higher" uses (i.e., avoids adverse social or ecological impacts and avoids competition with food production on the local, regional and/or global scale).
- Use secondary feedstock (i.e., recycled/waste-derived materials). Products are recycled into new materials with the goal to have equal quality and performance or higher (i.e., upcycling).

Design teams are invited to use this non-exhaustive list of sustainable design goals to guide their design process. Teams can add complementary sustainability design goals to this based on their own ambition level.

3.2. Factors Influencing the Definition and Implementation of the Sustainable Design Goals

Choosing the right sustainable design goals at the start of the material selection involves a variety of factors. The following factors influence how the sustainable design goals are identified and to what extent the designers and engineers' team have the ability reach these design goals.

3.2.1. Previous steps in the material selection process

As visualised in Figure 2.3, the definition and ranking of the sustainable design goals is based on the sustainable design principles mentioned in Chapter 1, design requirements defined by the designers and engineers earlier in the design process and the product concept that was consequently selected. Viability checks concerning the sustainable chemicals perspective include:

- **Sustainable design goals vs design requirements.** Sustainability design goals need to be compared with and evaluated against the design requirements that the team formulated earlier in the design process (see Chapter 2). Non-negotiable conditions set out in the design requirements have to be met by the to-be-designed product (i.e., needs). However, negotiable conditions deemed desirable for the to-be-designed product (i.e., wants) can be altered to meet the sustainable design goals.
- **Technical aspects** due to the product concept choice. What are the expected lifespan and durability of the product? What conditions will it have to resist (e.g. traffic, cleaning, etc.)?
- **Legal aspects** coming from the market chosen for the product. What are the compliance aspects to take into account? Think of for example international actions and national/regional regulations and restrictions for certain chemical substances, such as the Stockholm Convention, EU regulation for the Registration, Evaluation, Authorisation and Restriction of Chemicals (REACH) (No 1907/2006) and Directive 2011/65/EU on the restriction of the use of certain hazardous substances in electrical and electronic equipment. As chemical regulation is not static, consider regulatory horizon scanning in terms of anticipated or potential regulatory changes to avoid surprises. Does the product have to attain a certain certification (e.g. Cradle-to-Cradle Platinum certification determines the set of possible substances)?

- **Other aspects.** Does the designed product have to meet goals from voluntary industry initiatives? For instance, adhering to the European Plastic Pact leads to the target of reducing virgin plastic products by at least 20% (by weight) by 2025 with 10 % absolute reduction. In addition, are there specific procurement specifications?

3.2.2. The team

The team of designers and engineers (and beyond) is at the core of the design process. Sustainable chemistry aspects transpire within the team in different ways:

- **Cumulated knowledge on sustainability.** Are team members trained on sustainable design principles and life-cycle thinking?
- **Cumulated knowledge on chemistry.** Are team members trained on alternatives assessments, impact assessments tools, hazard/risk assessments and materials disclosure programmes?
- **Team objectives and values.** Is the team considering short term or long-term change (i.e., organisational and supply chain changes)? Are the team members likely to consider, test and develop radical and/or incremental innovative designs and polymer choices?

3.2.3. The context of the team's product design process

The team is influenced by the company context and the design brief:

- **The team's company.** What is the ambition level of the company when it comes to sustainability? Preferably, this is to pursue international best practices, aspire to inspire others, and collaborate across the value chain to strive for ambitious goals. To what extent is knowledge of sustainability and chemistry accessible within the group of company employees? What are internal existing circular infrastructures (e.g. refurbishment centre or takeback programme)? What is the latitude given to the team in terms of innovation (e.g. out of the box product concept or state of the art technologies) and organisational/supply chain change (e.g. collaborating with material suppliers or developing new system solutions)? Is it financially possible to invest in research and development for the integration of innovative product design, chemical substances and circular "waste" treatment structures? What are the geographical markets and channels to keep in mind?
- **Design brief.** What are the envisioned geographical markets and users? Will the product be a redesign or a completely new product? Is the product meant to be reused, refurbished, remanufactured and/or recycled?

3.3. Preparing to Deal with Future Trade-Offs

During the material selection process, the team is faced with trade-offs emerging from contradictory considerations throughout the life cycle of the product. To deal with these trade-offs, the sustainable design goals can be ranked by the team. Moreover, non-negotiable conditions can be drafted based on the sustainable design goals. Consideration should also be given to the potential for unintended consequences from material selection focused on a single application needing to work within an interdependent environment over its whole of life cycle.

3.3.1. Ranking sustainable design goals

The sustainable design goals can be ranked in order of importance for the design to help with weighing aspects of trade-offs.

The foundation of the ranking is compliance because the designed product will have to comply with the regulations relevant in the anticipated markets. The non-negotiable conditions from the design requirements will then have to be followed.

In terms of sustainable plastics, a certain prioritisation is made between and within sustainability and circularity factors. Note that circular solutions are not automatically sustainable (Geissdoerfer, Savaget, Bocken, and Hultink, 2016). The sustainability impact can be measured using a Life Cycle Assessment (LCA), which is standardised with ISO 14040 and 14044 (see Annex A: Overview of Relevant Methods, Tools and Metrics for specific methods and tools). The LCA indicators include global warming, eutrophication, acidification, damage to human health, damage to ecosystems and damage to resource availability. The field of circular economy incorporates the latter, which focuses on the increased extraction costs and energy costs. It complements it with maintaining the value and utility at a material, component, and product level at all times.

The circularity of solutions is measured using a variety of assessment methods (see Annex A: Overview of Relevant Methods, Tools and Metrics). This assessment is not yet standardised. ISO 59020 Measuring Circularity is expected in 2023. The position of recycling within the ranking varies depending on how circularity is measured by the team. One could consider the use of recycled plastics and recycling plastics at the end-of-use as a minimum requirement to limit the extraction of virgin materials and the loss of resources at the end-of-use. In contrast, one could choose not to prioritise recycling over other types of circular processing (e.g. repair and reuse) to focus on the extension of the lifetime of the product (Reikea, Vermeulen, and Witjes, 2018).

The ranking in Figure 3.1 is based on the former conceptualisation where closing resource loops is prioritised over slowing or narrowing resource loops. As mentioned earlier, the design team ideally already considered sustainability and circularity in the first stages of the design process, which resulted in design requirements already implementing sustainability and circularity. As this may not be the case in practice, Figure 3.1 explicitly incorporates sustainability and circularity between the non-negotiable design requirements (i.e., needs) and negotiable design requirements (i.e., wants) defined during the first stages of the design process.

Figure 3.1. Sustainable design goals ranking example if closing resource loops is prioritised over slowing and narrowing resource loops

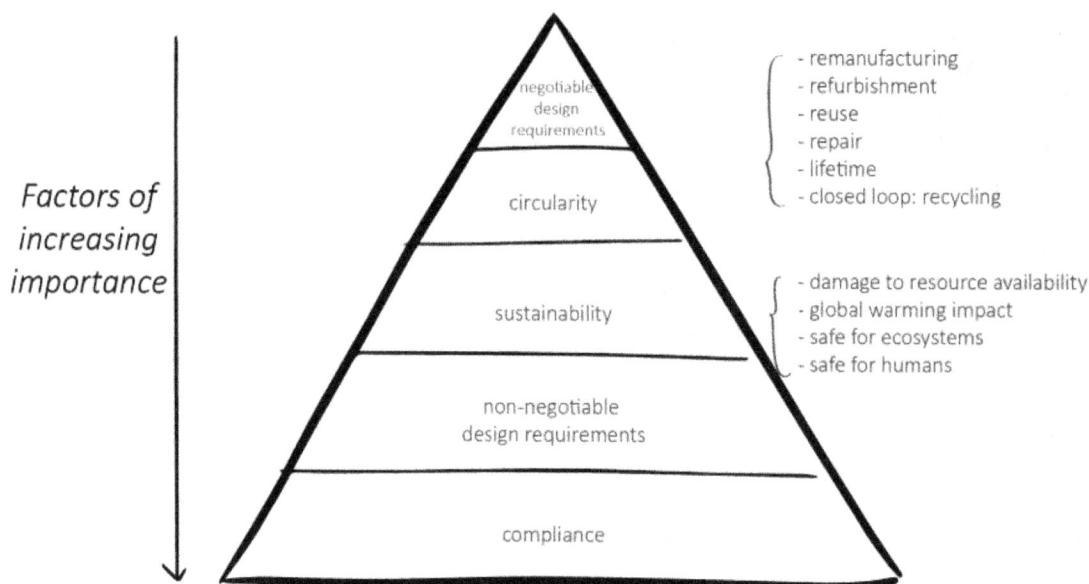

Factors of
increasing
importance

negotiable design requirements
- remanufacturing
- refurbishment
- reuse
- repair
- lifetime
- closed loop: recycling

circularity

sustainability
- damage to resource availability
- global warming impact
- safe for ecosystems
- safe for humans

non-negotiable design requirements

compliance

Ranked design goals (example)

1. Select materials with inherently low risk/hazard

2a. Use secondary feedstock or biobased feedstock

2b. Have a commercial 'afterlife' (recycling)

3. Generate no waste

4. Have a commercial 'afterlife' (other aspects)

3.3.2. Non-negotiable conditions based on the sustainable design goals

The design team has to decide what conditions are non-negotiable, preferably quantifying what has to be met for each goal. As a result, certain considerations can be evaluated as unacceptable if they fall under these conditions. For instance, a team may decide that it wishes to use as much recycled content as possible, but also that less than a specific amount of recycled content is unacceptable.

Now that the sustainable design goals have been defined and ranked, the considerations throughout the life cycle of the to-be-designed product to meet these sustainable design goals are explained in the following four chapters.

References

Geissdoerfer, M. et al. (2016), "The Circular Economy - A new sustainability paradigm?", *Journal of Cleaner Production*, Vol. 143, pp. 757-768.

OECD (2018a), "Considerations and criteria for sustainable plastics from a chemicals perspective: Background paper 1. OECD Global Forum on Environment: Plastics in a Circular Economy", *Series on Risk Management*, No. 51, OECD, Paris, https://www.oecd.org/chemicalsafety/risk-management/considerations-and-criteria-for-sustainable-plastics-from-a-chemicals-perspective.pdf

Reikea, D. et al. (2018), "The circular economy: New or Refurbished as CE 3.0? — Exploring Controversies in the Conceptualization of the Circular Economy through Focus on History and Resource Value Retention Options", *Resources, Conservation and Recycling*, Vol. 135, pp. 246-264.

.

Chapter 4. Considerations During the Sourcing Phase

This chapter focuses on the sourcing phase of the life-cycle and provides considerations for sustainable design from a chemicals perspective that are most relevant for this phase. Examples of trade-offs that arise in the sourcing phase are presented.

In the sourcing phase of the life cycle, the plastic pellets that will be used to make the product part are produced. Source materials include the primary chemicals and intermediates used to produce monomer(s) and catalysts/reagents/process chemicals. The sourcing phase includes the extraction of the feedstock and the production of the polymer. The sourcing considerations relevant for all types of products are as follows:

A. Select a base polymer (secondary or primary renewable source; secondary or primary non-renewable source) that:

- has the least emissions during extraction and production.
- uses non-hazardous or the least hazardous chemicals during extraction and production.
- minimises worker exposure during extraction and production.

B. Primary renewable feedstock (i.e., bio(based)plastics) is potentially a sustainable source, when:

- the benefits of using this feedstock, demonstrated through life-cycle assessment, outweigh the costs of externalities, such as water consumption, and competition with food production or social or ecological land use.
- the availability and continuity of availability of the supply of the feedstock enables its use.

C. Secondary feedstock is potentially a sustainable source, when:

- the propagation of hazardous chemicals is avoided.
- the resulting material contains a high percentage of the recycled material when designed.
- the current and future availability of the supply of the secondary feedstock enables its use.

D. Primary non-renewable feedstock can be used as last resort, if it minimises hazardous chemicals or hazardous mixtures of chemicals.

E. Strive for transparency in chemical compositions throughout the value chain.

Some of the above considerations, like emissions, are also relevant (and discussed) in the other lifecycle phases and should be considered holistically. A material that has lower emissions during extraction and production may end up having greater emissions at end-of-life or even across the whole life cycle. Feedstock selection should be informed by the benefits of matching the waste management operations in the intended market. If a material is bio-based and biodegradable for example, biodegradation/composting is a suitable choice, if the appropriate infrastructure is in place and if the material does not contain hazardous chemicals or hazardous chemical mixtures.

4.1. Considerations During the Sourcing Phase

In the following section, the considerations for the sourcing phase are further explained. Note that the considerations under A apply to the selection of all different sources: primary renewable feedstock (paragraph B), secondary feedstock (paragraph C) and primary non-renewable feedstock (paragraph D).

A. Select a base polymer (secondary or primary renewable source; secondary or primary non-renewable source) that:

- **has the least emissions during extraction and production.**

The extraction of the base polymer/source material and production of the polymer generate various emissions. "Waste" streams throughout this phase of the life cycle should be kept in the loop and at least recycled into another material. Emissions that cannot be kept in the loop should be specified (e.g. carbon dioxide (CO_2), methane and emissions harmful to human health and the environment). Tools to assess emissions during lifecycle phases are described in Annex A: Overview of Relevant Methods, Tools and Metrics.

- **uses non-hazardous or the least hazardous chemicals during extraction and production.**

Understanding the potential hazard(s) of chemicals in plastic types and possible exposure to these hazards enables design teams to select the most sustainable material options.

Hazards can emerge from the input chemicals and the production process (e.g. production residues, reaction products and other non-intentionally added substances).

Box 4.1. What can the design team do to prevent or minimise the use of hazardous chemicals at the sourcing phase

- Discuss potential hazards (i.e., primary chemicals, intermediates, monomers, and catalysts) with the supplier/producer.
  - *Tip: Note that there can be significant differences between production facilities for the same base polymer material. A series of Chemical Hazard Assessment methods and tools is provided in Annex A.*

- If hazardous source material is inevitable:
  - Prioritise suppliers that use a closed system to avoid exposure and disclose the use and release of chemicals of concern and express the desire for green chemistry solutions.
  - Re-evaluate the shortlist of polymers by asking if innovation is required on a material level.
    - *Tip: Tools for the substitution of safer chemicals are available (e.g. European Chemicals Agency or ECHA).*
  - Zoom out and re-evaluate the product design to consider whether another form of part/product could be chosen.

- **minimises worker exposure during extraction and production.**

During the sourcing phase, extraction and production workers can be exposed to hazardous chemicals. Exposure depends on a variety of factors such as physical and chemical properties, its volume and production conditions.

B. **Primary renewable feedstock (i.e., bio(based)plastics) is potentially a sustainable source, when:**

- **the benefits of using this feedstock, demonstrated through life-cycle assessment, outweigh the costs of externalities, such as water consumption, and competition with food production or social or ecological land use.**

The chosen polymer(s) for the product part has one of three sources: primary renewable feedstock, secondary or recycled feedstock (paragraph C) or primary non-renewable feedstock (paragraph D).

A resource is considered renewable when the regeneration is able to keep up with the extraction and consumption of the material. Rapidly renewable resources are selected to decouple feedstock extraction from fossil resources and reduce the emission of greenhouse gasses. The feedstock is not considered sustainable when it requires the destruction of natural capital (e.g. deforestation of rainforests to gain arable land). The cultivation of crops for plastic production should also not compete with pharmaceutical or food production in areas where arable land or water is scarce, or crop yields are unstable. By-products or residues of food production can be selected as feedstock in these cases.

Furthermore, if the cultivation of the feedstock heavily depends on fossil-based energy, through petrol for tractors or on the use of fertilizers, use of hazardous substances such as pesticides, or large amounts of fresh water, the overall environmental impact of the feedstock might be higher than that of fossil-based alternatives. Therefore, renewable feedstocks should always be evaluated for their full Life Cycle Assessment (LCA) and economic and social impact. Credible third-party certification can provide a direction to the design team in the selection of sustainable renewable feedstock. See Annex A: Overview of Relevant Methods, Tools and Metrics.

- **the current and future availability of the supply of feedstock enables its use.**

A certain continuity of the sourcing of the feedstock is needed to invest in research and development throughout the supply chain. An extra difficulty for renewable feedstock is the need to deal with more extreme seasonal differences, so risk spreading or the use of a combination of several sources is an important factor to take into account.

C. Secondary feedstock is potentially a sustainable source, when:

The use of secondary feedstock, or recycled plastics, generally decreases the environmental and health impact of material production, prevents waste, and incentivises collection and recycling of the plastic at end-of-use.

- **the propagation of hazardous chemicals is avoided.**

Be mindful of possible hazardous chemicals coming from production residues (e.g. monomers, oligomers and catalysts), additives (e.g. impact modifiers and pigments), non-intentionally added substances (e.g. side products or degradation products) and legacy chemicals from previous uses (e.g. residual inks and adhesives in secondary feedstock). Choosing mechanically recycled plastics can be challenging as information on their chemical content is often unavailable. In chemical recycling, there is the possibility to capture and remove the so-called "legacy" chemical additives and chemicals of concern that may be present in discarded plastics. However, chemical recycling is relatively immature and not a widespread option. Further, the energy instensity of available chemical recycling processes raises concerns for the environmental impacts and benefits of chemical recycling. In both cases, reliable material streams where the producer has considerable control over the process are preferred.

Suppliers should always be asked for material screening to identify hazardous chemicals and reasonably expected NIAS. The absence of hazardous chemicals in the feedstock should be ensured.

- **the resulting material contains a high percentage of the recycled material when designed.**

The design team could aim for the highest percentage of recycled material possible when there are no legislative limits on percentages of recycled content. The use of recycled plastic in a new product increases the demand for recycled plastics, which in turn creates an incentive for collection and recycling at end-of-use.

A knowledge gap exists in current material databases. Virgin plastic grades are not the same as recycled grades. Find out which material can fulfil the design requirements, and then check with material experts whether the corresponding recycled material is suitable. Design from Recycling guidelines developed by PolyCE could be used to inform this (PolyCE, 2021). Also, check with manufacturing process experts as to how much recycled content can be used in a given application and on existing processing equipment.

- **the current and future availability of the supply of the secondary feedstock enables its use.**

The availability of recycling infrastructure varies globally and, therefore, so does the availability of recycled feedstock. In addition, affordability impacts access especially when market prices for primary non-renewable feedstock are cheaper than secondary feedstock, which has sometimes been the case.

Note that the grade of the recycled content should match the 'grade' of the application of the plastic product. As food grade recycled plastic availability is limited, it should not be employed in applications that do not have a food grade requirement.

D. Primary non-renewable feedstock can be used as last resort, if:

Primary non-renewable feedstock, or "virgin plastic", should only be used when renewable and secondary feedstock cannot be used. Its use is not sustainable as it requires the extraction of finite resources and inherently means that already extracted resources are not employed. The chosen primary non-renewable plastic should at least be readily reusable or recyclable (preferably retaining its quality, i.e., excluding downcycling), especially when the lifetime of the product is short.

- **it minimises hazardous chemicals or hazardous mixtures of chemicals.**

If the use of virgin plastics is not completely avoidable/substitutable (e.g. as a combination is needed with recycled content to attain certain specifications), virgin resin may pose a toxicity risk to human health or biodiversity, just as recycled plastics. Hazardous chemicals could emerge from production residues (e.g. monomers, oligomers, catalysts), additives (e.g. flame retardants, heat and oxidation stabilisers, and pigments), and NIAS (e.g. due to degradation). Virgin plastics that minimise hazardous chemicals or hazardous mixtures of chemicals should be used.

Box 4.2. Example of sourcing phase considerations in the packaging sector

In food-contact applications such as biscuit packaging, the application of plastics from secondary feedstock is limited. Food safety regulations prohibit the use of plastics with risks of contamination in food-contact applications because contamination with hazardous chemicals is difficult to exclude. Processes exist to guide the certification of food contact grade plastics including those from recycled source materials. Consult the OECD case studies (OECD, 2021c; OECD, 2021d) for an evaluation of polymers from renewable feedstock (i.e., BioPE (polyethylene), BioPP (polypropylene), BioPET (polyethylene terephthalate), PLA (polylactic acid) and regenerated cellulose) and secondary feedstock (i.e., recycled LDPE (low density PE), recycled HDPE (high density PE), recycled PP, recycled PET, PA (polyamide), PLA, and regenerated cellulose) according to these considerations. These case studies outline considerations of certain polymers and additives for the design of packaging.

E. Strive for transparency in chemical compositions throughout the value chain.

To support (more) informed decision-making concerning the chemicals used in manufacturing, as much transparency as possible is important to identify what is known and where data gaps lie. Unfortunately, the composition of all materials is not typically fully known, nor are hazard data complete, but designers are trained to work with uncertainties. Relevant information on chemical composition (and its effect on health and the environment, i.e. hazard data) should also be passed along the value chain so that manufacturers, governments, users, consumers and recyclers have efficient access to information. Information on product composition should be kept available for at least the entire life span of the product, after products are marketed. Ideally, this information could be retained and auditable at each stage. Designers can consider material passports at chemical level. Blockchain with chemical markers, watermarks or QR codes are possible solutions.

4.2. Trade-Offs within the Sourcing Phase

Table 4.1. Various trade-offs emerging from taking sourcing phase considerations into account

Lowest emissions during extraction and production	vs	Use of secondary feedstock

Secondary feedstock generally decreases the environmental impact of material production, but due to legacy chemicals they potentially could emit hazardous volatile organic compounds (VOCs) during production.

Lowest (exposure to) hazardous chemicals during extraction and production	vs	Use of secondary feedstock

Secondary feedstock generally decreases the environmental impact of material production, but there is a risk for legacy hazardous chemicals. Choosing recycled plastics can be challenging because information is often lacking on the chemicals in the plastics. Previous use cycles may have included toxic additives or other additives that are undesirable for the next use cycle. Information also is lacking on how well different plastics undergo multiple cycles. For Packaging Plastics this information is available (Schyns, 2021).

Lowest emissions during extraction and production	vs	Lowest emissions during the whole life cycle

Polymers with the least emissions during extraction and production may not necessarily deliver the greatest carbon abatement outcome over the whole life cycle. The alternative with the greatest carbon abatement outcome should be selected.

Reduced material use	vs	Use of fewer material types

A designer should consider the trade-off between use of an extra component (e.g. addition of a heat sealable layer to a film) and that of reduced material use (e.g. when using an oriented film).

Reduced material use	vs	Close material loops

Light weighting of products to reduce material use might require polymers of virgin quality. However, to effectively close material loops, recycled content in products should be maximised, possibly leading to heavier designs.
Furthermore, certain polymers require less material in production (e.g. PET in bottles compared to HDPE bottles) but are sourced from a scarce stream (e.g. food grade recycled PET).

Reduced material use	vs	Reduced virgin resin use

Due to lower quality of recycled plastic, products may have increased thickness to meet product requirements, so they use more plastic, are heavier, but (should) have the advantage of using less virgin plastic.

Cost of value chain	vs	Benefits of value chain

Many virgin polymers come from long and established value chains, whereas new secondary or renewable feedstock come from shorter chains, where knowledge gaps emerge regarding hazards.
Conversely, it could also be that an inexpensive polymer has a complex and long value chain, while a more expensive polymer has a clear short value chain with few hazards.

References

OECD (2021c), "Case Study on Detergent Bottles; An example of weighing sustainability criteria for rigid plastic non-food packaging", *Series on Risk Management*, No. 63, OECD, Paris.

OECD (2021d), "Case Study on Biscuit Wrappers; An example of weighing sustainability criteria for plastic flexible food packaging from a chemicals perspective", *Series on Risk Management*, No. 64, OECD, Paris.

PolyCE (2021), *Design for Recycling Design from Recycling - Practical guidelines for designers*. Post-

Consumer High-tech Recycled Polymers for a Circular Economy – European Commission Funded Project, ISBN 978-90-813418-0-6, https://www.polyce-project.eu/wp-content/uploads/2021/04/PolyCE-E-book-Circular-Design-Guidelines-2.pdf

Schyns, Z. O. G. and M. P. Shaver (2021), "Mechanical Recycling of Packaging Plastics: A Review." *Macromolecular Rapid Communications*, Vol. 42, No. 3, pp. 2000415.

Chapter 5. Considerations During the Manufacturing Phase

This chapter focuses on the manufacturing phase of the life-cycle and provides considerations for sustainable design from a chemicals perspective that are most relevant for this phase. Examples of trade-offs that arise in the manufacturing phase are presented.

During the manufacturing phase of the life cycle, the plastic granulates are made into a product part. Common chemical types used in the process are raw materials, monomers, oligomers, catalysts, polymers, performance additives (e.g. anti-oxidants, colorants, plasticisers, UV stabilisers, flame retardants, compatibilisers, etc.), and manufacturing and processing aids (e.g. lubricants, anti-block and slipping agents, and antistatic agents). Several considerations need to be taken into account throughout the manufacturing phase:

A. Select a manufacturing technique that:
- generates the least emissions.
- uses the least processing aids.
- uses non-hazardous or the least hazardous chemicals.
- minimises worker exposure.

B. Consider sustainable manufacturing on a systems level.

C. Ensure transparency in chemical composition throughout the value chain.

5.1. Considerations during the Manufacturing Phase

In this section, the considerations for the manufacturing phase are further explained.

A. Select a manufacturing technique that:
- **generates the least emissions.**

Manufacturing plastic products can generate various emissions. "Waste" streams throughout this phase of the life cycle should be kept in the loop and at least recycled into another material. Emissions that cannot be kept in the loop should be specified (e.g. CO_2, methane, and emissions harmful to human health and the environment). Tools to assess emissions during lifecycle phases are described in Annex A: Overview of Relevant Methods, Tools and Metrics.

Consider the emissions calculated with life cycle analysis for diverse manufacturing techniques to compare them. Consult the OECD case study on detergent packaging to learn more about the sustainability of extrusion blow moulding compared to injection stretch blow moulding (OECD, 2021d).

- **uses the least processing aids.**

Find a manufacturing technique that minimises the variety of types of chemicals and their quantity required to abate the consequent environmental pollution and human exposure. Moreover, consider the energy consumption (i.e., amount and source of energy), water consumption and overall waste produced to compare manufacturing techniques.

Questions to ask suppliers and producers: What chemicals are used as processing aids and in what quantity? Are the facilities tracking their emissions and their energy, water, and material use? Have they set goals to reduce these?

- **uses non-hazardous or the least hazardous chemicals.**

Consideration of chemical hazards are key when designing sustainable plastic products. Chemicals needed during the manufacturing processes and that will be present in the finished plastic article should first be identified. Their hazards and particular properties (e.g. persistency or mobility in the environment, potential to bioaccumulate) should assessed. Use of chemicals that are, for example: carcinogenic, mutagenic, or toxic to reproduction (CMR), Persistent, Bioaccumulative and/or Toxic (PBT), very Persistent and very Bioaccumulative (vPvB), Persistent, Mobile, and Toxic (PMT) or are of other concern, such as Endocrine-Disrupting Chemicals (EDC) should be avoided.

The use scenarios for a product define the requirements for manufacturing techniques, as well as all the other life cycle phases. With products that come into close contact with food or skin (e.g. food packaging, toys) particular efforts are warranted, such as not using any hazardous substances.

Box 5.1. What can the design team do to prevent or minimise the use of hazardous chemicals at the manufacturing phase

- Consider and compare manufacturing processes based on their possibility to minimise the use and release of hazardous chemicals and pollution.
    - *Tips: Be aware that a chemical inventory is limited by current knowledge. Currently not all additives and non-intentionally added substances (NIAS) can be identified. Diverse assessment methods, each with their own data needs, can be applied (see Annex A). Also, do not only consider currently regulated substances, take future regulatory actions on emerging chemicals of concern into account when possible.*
    - *The OECD created the Substitution and Alternatives Assessment Tool Selector enabling designers to evaluate the most suitable hazard assessment tool.*
- Consider whether the function of that chemical is crucial for product performance and remove if possible.
- If it cannot be removed, find alternatives for hazardous chemicals.
    - *Tip: Check guidance (OECD, 2021; ECHA, n.d.)*
- If no alternatives to hazardous chemicals were found:
    - Seek a supply chain where the desire for environmentally conscious chemistry solutions was expressed.
        - *Tips: Consider how stringent the legislation on hazardous chemicals is at the manufacturing location. Regulation that is more lenient will lead to more risks in the supply chain.*
        - *Questions to ask suppliers and manufacturers:*
            - *Are the facilities tracking the use of all chemicals (particularly hazardous chemicals) throughout the manufacturing process? This includes chemicals composing the product (both polymer and additives), as well as processing aids.*
            - *Are the facilities tracking the release of all chemicals (particularly hazardous chemicals), including compliance with waste regulations?*
            - *Are the facilities reporting this information along the value chain?*
            - *Have the facilities set goals for eliminating or reducing the use and release of hazardous chemicals?*
    - Re-evaluate the shortlist of polymers: is innovation on a material level required?
    - Zoom out and re-evaluate the product design to consider whether another form of part/product could be chosen.

- **minimises worker exposure.**

Consider what exposure scenarios are to be expected during the manufacturing processes studied.

Prioritise consideration of occupational and environmental exposures to hazardous chemicals, and toxic emissions and waste. Comparative exposure mapping helps to pinpoint potential exposure pathways. Qualitative exposure assessments can be based on the presence of chemicals in a form that can be inhaled, ingested or absorbed through the skin during the manufacturing of the product part.

Box 5.2. Example of a construction sector-specific consideration concerning exposure during manufacturing

Consider the risk of monomer exposure for closed cell rigid foam manufacturing, because the polymer is formed during this process. In contrast, polystyrene insulation is made from the polymer. Consult the OECD case study (OECD, 2021b) for an evaluation of manufacturing processes for four types of plastic insulation.

B. Consider sustainable manufacturing on a systems level

It is important to take into account the environmental impacts associated with the manufacture and distribution of products. For example, if a product consists of different parts that are to be mounted together, consider a physical design of parts to avoid the need of glue. By such design choices, additional chemicals can be avoided and the product will more easily be reused or recycled. For transport, consider the distance between the manufacturing facility where product parts are made and the location where they are assembled or completed (e.g. filling a bottle of detergent). Ideally, these processes occur at the same location, with limited distance to retailers. When this is not possible at the same location, another manufacturing technique could be considered. For instance, it is recommended to assess the environmental impact of transporting empty bottles to be filled versus reheating preforms for injection stretch blow moulding on location.

Question to suppliers or manufacturers: what measures are in place to track and report key sustainability measures?

C. Ensure transparency in chemical composition throughout the value chain.

To support informed decision-making concerning the chemicals used in manufacturing, transparency is important to identify what is known and where data gaps lie. A tiered and iterative approach to chemicals inventory could be used (i.e., "starting with higher disclosure thresholds, and working to gather additional information at lower thresholds as feasible and relevant").

For example, the Global Automotive Declarable Substance List (GADSL) can be used to assess substances expected to be present in automotive products through the supply chain.

5.2. Trade-Offs within the Manufacturing Phase

Table 5.1. Various trade-offs emerging from taking manufacturing phase considerations into account

Benefits of efficient manufacture	vs	Consequences of the required additives on hazard, energy/water/material use
Certain additives (like anti-static agents) can ease or speed up the manufacturing process, but consequently require more material use or create hazards.		
Known hazardous chemical	**vs**	**Uncertain hazard of chemical**
Even if chemical contents are known, most chemicals do not currently have full hazard assessments, meaning data gaps exist in one or more hazard endpoints. A design team may have to choose between a chemical that is known to be hazardous and a chemical that is not known to be hazardous but has gaps in hazard data.		
Reduce material use	**vs**	**Reduce hazards**
Certain plastics (like insulation materials) are very efficient in volume, mass or thickness, but contain more potential hazardous substances in compared with less efficient materials. While resource efficiency is important and frequently has direct economic implications (e.g. energy consumption), it is important that designers consider resource efficiency metrics separately from metrics that address exposure to human health or environmental hazards. They are linked to different sustainable design principles and should not be aggregated.		
Benefits of increased performance	**vs**	**Consequences of the required additives on hazard, energy/water/material use**
Increased product complexity or additives included to improve performance should be considered in terms of the potential trade-offs for other life cycle stages. Innovative product design or additives, or complete reimagining of the materials that make up the product, can be used to maintain or increase performance without increasing hazards or introducing other environmental impacts.		

References

ECHA. (n.d.). *Substances of concern: Why and how to substitute?* European Chemicals Agency, Helsinki, Finland, https://echa.europa.eu/documents/10162/24152346/why_and_how_to_substitute_en.pdf/93e9c055-483c-743a-52cb-1d1201478bc1

OECD (2021), "Guidance on Key Considerations for the Identification and Selection of Safer Chemical Alternative", *Series on Risk Management*, No.60, OECD, Paris, https://www.oecd.org/chemicalsafety/risk-management/guidance-on-key-considerations-for-the-identification-and-selection-of-safer-chemical-alternatives.pdf

OECD (2021b), "Case Study on Insulation: An example of chemical considerations for sustainable plastics design", *Series on Risk Management*, No.66, OECD, Paris.

OECD (2021d), "Case Study on Biscuit Wrappers; An example of weighing sustainability criteria for plastic flexible food packaging from a chemicals perspective", *Series on Risk Management*, No. 64, OECD, Paris.

Chapter 6. Considerations During the Use Phase

This chapter focuses on the use phase of the life-cycle and provides considerations for sustainable design from a chemicals perspective that are most relevant for this phase. Examples of trade-offs that arise in the use phase are presented.

In the use phase, the plastic product is acquired by a user and consequently utilised. Users could be exposed to substances above levels considered harmful during the use of the plastic product. These substances could be emitted by the product itself or by maintenance products needed during the lifespan of the product. From a designers' perspective, the material selection journey starts with the use phase as the functionality of the product depends on its purpose during use and its use context. The considerations at the use phase are as follows.

A. Consider whether the determined chemical and mechanical requirements are strict, or there is flexibility to allow for more sustainable choices.

B. Select a base polymer/source material that:
- generates the least emissions.
- prevents or minimises exposure to hazardous chemicals during use and maintenance.
- enables the intended lifespan of the product.

C. Map exposure scenarios during use and reduce exposure to hazard as much as possible.

6.1. Considerations during the Use Phase

In this section, the considerations for the use phase are further explained.

A. Consider whether the determined chemical and mechanical requirements are strict, or there is flexibility to allow for more sustainable choices.

The determined chemical and mechanical requirements can be restrictive to genuinely sustainable chemical selection and material innovation. These requirements might be set with safety margins of a supplier in addition to safety margins of a manufacturer, making them excessive or they might include requirements that are tentative in nature. Consider whether the requirements are unnecessarily restrictive in relation to the intended use of the product.

B. Select a base polymer/source material that:
- **generates the least emissions.**

For plastic products that are continuously transported during their lifespan, plastics with lower densities or foamed plastics can be considered to reduce CO_2 emissions and consequently fuel use. For plastic packaging, always consider the use phase of its content. If the packaging is to be used as food packaging, then shelf life should be considered as one of the most important factors for prevention of food waste. In addition, other spoilage of content should always be prevented with the choice of the right type of polymer and additives. Furthermore, the shedding of microplastics or microfibres during use of the product should be prevented.

Box 6.1. Examples of a transportation and agriculture sector-specific considerations during the use phase

Transportation: Consider impact of light-weighting on fuel use; consider the dispersion of microplastics by vehicles' tyres. For plastic products that are continuously transported during their lifespan, plastics with lower densities or foamed plastics can be considered to reduce CO_2 emissions.

Agriculture: Due to high risks of littering and loss of films (or parts of films) or clips used in agriculture, soil degradable plastics can be considered for use (e.g. for applications like mulch films). However, caution may be needed even if soil degradable plastic is chosen. Under certain conditions it does not degrade for a very long time and can also disperse chemicals into the environment.

- **prevents or minimises exposure to hazardous chemicals during use and maintenance.**

Consumers or professional users can be exposed to hazardous chemicals or volatile organic compounds (VOCs) emitted during the use or maintenance of the product. Exposure depends on a variety of factors such as the type of contact with the product (e.g. skin contact, food contact). Hazards can emerge from the input chemicals, the production process (e.g. production residues, reaction products and non-intentionally added substances (NIAS), and from the conditions in which the product is being used or maintained (e.g. temperature, the way it reacts to cleaning agents). These hazards should be discussed with the supplier/producer.

- **enables the intended lifespan of the product.**

The use phase of products can range from seconds to half centuries. Usually expensive, high-end engineering plastics are not used for packaging that is rapidly disposed of. However, designers should consider that multiple recycling loops affect the quality of polymers and that it could be beneficial in the long term to use higher quality polymers for products that have long lifespans as well as products that are recycled very often. In addition, polymer quality can be maintained during multiple recycling loops by using techniques that can counter degradation and also due to the typically heterogeneous nature of the source of input materials. Moreover, some plastics are recycled differently than others. PET, for instance, can be recycled about eight times before a noticeable degradation in quality takes place due to chain length shortening.

C. Map exposure scenarios during use and reduce exposure to hazard as much as possible.

Study the use context of the plastic product. How does the use alter the product after manufacturing (e.g. installation, tear and wear, heating)? Consequently, consider the risks linked to these types of exposures. For example, chemical leaching, microplastic shedding and degradation of the product with time could expose users and the environment to harmful chemicals. Hazards associated with plastics are often linked to non-polymeric substances such as unreacted monomers, partially reacted oligomers or additives. Together with the supplier, identify the molecular weight ranges of production residues. Lower molecular weight will make chemicals more likely to migrate and more easily gain entry into biological systems. Molecules of 1 000 Daltons are considered as immobile in this respect.

Determine if microplastics or fibres will be directly released into wastewater during use, or microplastics expected to shed from the product during use/washing. To reduce this exposure, consider how (important) information about the chemical composition of the plastic and relevant control measures could be conveyed to the user.

Although the priority remains on expected use scenarios, consider the exposure under plausible misuse and worst-case scenarios.

6.2. Trade-Offs within the Use Phase

Table 6.1. Various trade-offs emerging from taking use phase considerations into account

Prevention of maintenance aids	vs	Uncertain chemical hazard
Nano chemicals can be used to create surfaces to which dirt cannot attach itself, so no cleaning agents or sometimes extra paint layers are necessary. However, these chemicals might have gaps in hazard data.		
Waste created	vs	**Waste avoided**
The waste created from the plastic in a packaging application vs the waste of the product it contains. For example, weigh the impact of plastics vs impact of food waste.		
Low emissions	vs	**Low maintenance**
Certain plastics require low or no maintenance but emit VOCs during the use phase.		
Low emissions	vs	**Long lifespan**
Certain plastics (like soft PVC) have a long lifespan but emit VOCs or other particles during the use phase.		
Reduce weight	vs	**Efficiency of transport**
Foamed plastics will weigh less but may take up a lot of space and thus require more shipments for the same functional unit.		

Chapter 7. Considerations During the End-of-Use Phase

This chapter focuses on the end-of-use phase of the life-cycle and provides considerations for sustainable design from a chemicals perspective that are most relevant for this phase. Examples of trade-offs that arise in the end-of-use phase are presented.

During the end-of-use phase, the user dispenses with the plastic product, after which it is ideally collected, sorted and treated. The following considerations need to be taken into account.

A. Minimise the amount of waste at end-of-use through polymer selection.

B. Simplify designs to include as few different polymers as possible.

C. Maximise the production of high-quality recycled materials as output of the recycling process.

D. Minimise the amount of and exposure to chemical hazard at end-of-use through chemical selection.

E. Match the polymer selection to the waste management operations in the intended market.

F. Consider ways to mitigate the risk of littering.

G. Ensure transparency of chemical composition

7.1. Considerations during the End-of-Use Phase

In this section, the considerations for the end-of-use phase are further explained.

A. Minimise the amount of waste at end-of-use through polymer selection.

In a circular economy, resources are kept at their highest value and utility at all times. As a result, at the end-of-use, reuse, refurbishment, remanufacture and - at least – recycling should be enabled. Incineration and landfill should be avoided as much as possible (Ellen MacArthur Foundation, 2013). Therefore, to minimise the amount of waste at end-of-use, select polymers that are known to be collected, sorted, and at least recycled for the applicable product type in the intended market. For instance, for collected household appliances (white goods) in Western Europe, the polymers acrylonitrile-butadiene-styrene (ABS), high-impact polystyrene and polycarbonate are known to be sorted and recycled. Before introducing new polymers, that could have benefits in other life cycle phases, plans should be made for an appropriate sorting and recycling infrastructure.

B. Simplify designs to include as few different polymers as possible.

Next to using well-recycled polymers in a product, product designs should be simplified to include as few different polymers as possible in order to prevent contamination and mixed waste streams, which lead to large amounts of potentially recyclable polymers not being recycled. Although out of scope for this report, note the importance of the product design as mentioned in Chapter 2. Teams should consider if the product design facilitates maximum recovery and recycling of the materials. For example, if a product consists of different parts that are to be mounted together, consider a physical design of parts to avoid the need of glue. By such design choices, additional chemicals can be avoided and the product will more easily be reused or recycled.

Take the value of the recycled material into account. Consider if the design facilitates repair, reuse or disassembly. This includes conveying information on the chemical content of the product.

C. Maximise the production of high-quality recycled materials as output of the recycling process.

Use recyclable materials which will be recycled at the highest quality possible to become future secondary feedstock and close the loop (possibly product-to-product). There are several guidelines available to assess the recyclability of polymers used in packaging (See Annex A: Overview of Relevant Methods, Tools and Metrics).

Currently, most recycling processes are mechanical recycling processes, in which the plastics products or packaging are usually sorted, shredded, washed, and extruded to create granulate for new compounds. Presently, plastics containing certain additives (like fibreglass) or highly contaminated materials cannot be recycled mechanically into high quality recycled grades that can be used in the same applications they once were (TNO, 2021).

In this context, thermoplastics are generally easier to recycle at a high quality than thermosets.

Note that in the future, chemical recycling is likely to develop rapidly. However, bringing resources back to molecular level requires a lot of energy. Therefore, it is expected to still co-exist with mechanical recycling which is more energy efficient.

Plastics as fuel seems detrimental in geographic regions with both good waste management infrastructure and access to fuel. Nevertheless, it may have various social and environmental benefits in regions where these resources are lacking (i.e., reducing litter and providing fuel for cooking and tractors while avoiding cutting down trees). Although out of scope for this report, be mindful of social contexts.

Box 7.1. Examples specific considerations for the electrical and electronic equipment and automotive sectors during the end-of-use phase

Electrical and electronic equipment (EEE) sector: The EU's Waste Electrical and Electronic Equipment (WEEE) directive prohibits the disposal of EEE in household waste and promotes the separated collection of these products. Consider design for easy separation of each part in EEE. Mark parts to distinguish the polymer type.

Automotive sector: If safety and durability during use allow it, avoid using reinforced materials such as glass fibre, which cause difficulty for recycling.

D. Minimise the amount of and exposure to chemical hazard at end-of-use through chemical selection.

In the recycling process, the plastics will be shredded and re-melted. In this process, thermal degradation products are formed. The nature and amount of volatile organic compounds (VOCs) formed depend on the polymer type. In the example of polymers in household appliances, it can be noted that acrylonitrile-butadiene-styrene (ABS) and polystyrene will emit far more VOCs than polycarbonate (He, et al., 2015).

Chemical additives in plastics create their own degradation products during recycling and incineration. During incineration, the presence of flame-retardants in household products, for instance halogenated flame-retardants, can lead to the emission of dioxins and dioxin-like compounds.

Chemical additives can also create chemical hazards in landfills or unofficial disposal. Chemicals will leach from plastic products into the environment. Cadmium stabilisers used in the past in PVC construction products increase the lifespan of the product but are carcinogenic and toxic for aquatic lifeforms. Other PVC concerns include leaching of lead and phthalates. The exposure of workers to chemical hazards during collection, disassembly, shredding and repair should be prevented or minimised.

The use of substances that create hazardous degradation products or legacy chemicals in the recycled material should be avoided. The following two design guidelines can help prevent the exposure to chemical hazards from batteries or other hazardous components:

- Enable easy access and removal of hazardous or polluting components.
- Use material combinations and connections that allow easy liberation.

E. Match the polymer selection to the waste management operations in the intended market.

Every country, region or sometimes municipality has their own waste management system.

Feedstock selection benefits from matching to the end-of-life fate. If a material is a biodegradable/compostable plastic, for example, biodegradation/composting is a suitable fate. It is essential that design decisions take into account the actual outcomes (i.e. something is actually composted or biodegraded, with the appropriate infrastructure already in place) instead of their potential (compostable or biodegradable). If the selected end-of-life option is biodegradation or composting, ensure the absence of hazardous chemicals or hazardous chemical mixtures in the finished plastic, especially if they are persistent, as such chemicals will not degrade and will be dispersed when the plastics itself degrades. For products with long lifespans, consider developments in waste management and recycling technology.

F. Consider ways to mitigate the risk of littering.

In specific situations, where accidental littering (or shedding of microplastics) cannot be avoided, biodegradable, soil degradable or water-soluble plastics could be considered. However, at this moment, most biodegradable polymers can only degrade in industrial composting facilities; they will not degrade in the environment. Because labelling a product as "biodegradable" could increase the likelihood of littering behaviour, efforts should be made to improve awareness about proper disposal. An additional issue with littering of plastics is that there is also the risk of hazardous chemicals dispersing to the environment from the littered product.

G. Ensure transparency of chemical composition.

Information about the chemical composition should reach waste management services. Designers can consider material passports at chemical level. Blockchain with chemical markers, watermarks or QR codes are possible solutions. As a part of European Sustainable Product Initiative there is development of a digital product pass including information (also chemicals) for the value chain and information to consumers.

7.2. Trade-Offs within the End-of-Use

Table 7.1. Various trade-offs emerging from taking end-of-use considerations into account

Material innovation	vs	Availability of recycling infrastructure
Innovative materials which may be more sustainable usually do not have a recycling infrastructure in place. Bringing a new material to the market brings a responsibility in the adjustment (or creation) of the recycling infrastructure needed.		
Simplify designs	**vs**	**Usability and desirability**
Simplifying designs by including as few different polymers as possible could impact the aesthetics of the product or even the usability of a product, for instance by avoiding soft-touch handgrips in beer crates. But they can be easier to recycle.		
Low transport emissions	**vs**	**Recycling**
The availability of recycling infrastructure varies globally. Transporting materials long distances for recycling can lead to additional life cycle impacts that would need to be considered when reviewing trade-offs of mechanical or chemical recycling. In the design process, using inherently low hazard additives and mechanically recyclable plastics, along with programs to develop the necessary infrastructure, can foster a closed-loop system.		
Including in recycling streams	**vs**	**Permanent disposal**
"Dealing with legacy products, some of which contain chemicals of concern, versus new products containing safer chemicals is also a challenge. Products with highly hazardous or banned chemicals already on the market should be treated separately from newer material streams, and recycling may not be the best option. Trade-offs between permanent disposal, instead of inclusion in recycling streams, will need to be considered." (OECD, 2018a).		

References

Ellen MacArthur Foundation (2013), *Towards the circular economy. Volume 1: Economic and business rationale for an accelerated transition*, United Kingdom, https://ellenmacarthurfoundation.org/towards-the-circular-economy-vol-1-an-economic-and-business-rationale-for-an

He, et al. (2015), "Pollution characteristics and health risk assessment of volatile organic compounds emitted from different plastic solid waste recycling workshops", Vol. 77, pp. 85–94.

OECD (2018a), "Considerations and criteria for sustainable plastics from a chemicals perspective: Background paper 1. OECD Global Forum on Environment: Plastics in a Circular Economy", *Series on Risk Management*, No. 51, OECD, Paris, https://www.oecd.org/chemicalsafety/risk-management/considerations-and-criteria-for-sustainable-plastics-from-a-chemicals-perspective.pdf

TNO (2021), *A circular economy for plastics*, Brochure of the Netherlands Organization for Applied Scientific Research, Netherlands, https://publications.tno.nl/publication/34637978/cSKNrZ/TNO-2021-circular.pdf

Chapter 8. Whole Product Assessment and Optimisation

This chapter brings together the considerations highlighted across the various life-cycle phases in order to consider whole product assessment and optimisation of the design. When doing so, trade-offs emerge between the life cycle phases and examples of these are presented.

After looking at every phase of the life cycle separately, designers and engineers need to combine the considerations from every phase. When doing so, trade-offs emerge between the life cycle phases.

The material selection can be optimised for the sustainable design goals. The design team should look for dominance in options (i.e., win-win situations). This chapter identifies the resulting trade-offs and illustrates how to deal with them.

8.1. Trade-Offs between Life Cycle Phases

The decisions or constraints in one phase of the life cycle influence the possibilities in the other phases. Table 8.1 indicates how constraints set in the top row of the table influence the phases in the column on the left. The list is non-exhaustive and should be complemented by the design team.

Table 8.1. Dependencies between decisions and constraints in one life cycle phase to the other phases

How Influences	Sourcing	Manufacturing	Use	End-of-Use
Sourcing		- A selected production method requires specific feedstock. - A selected production method requires the use of specific additives.	- Non-negotiable design requirements (e.g. function of the product, food safety, barrier properties and chemical resistance) limit sourcing options.	- Aiming for product-to-product recycling limits the polymer and sourcing options. - A preferred end-of-use scenario limits the number of possible materials. - Recycled content vs recyclability.
Manufacturing	- Available polymers might require specific production methods and additives.		- Non-negotiable design requirements (e.g. function of the product) can lead to production residues to which installers are exposed. These could have been avoided at the production phase if the requirement was negotiable. - Non-negotiable design requirements (e.g. barrier properties) may require bonding of multiple materials.	- Sorting and mechanical recycling depends on the product design. - Recycling or composting preference limits the material options during manufacturing.
Use	- Properties of the available materials might not meet design requirements. - Some plastics emit hazardous volatile organic compounds (VOCs) during their sourcing process, but current alternatives without hazardous VOCs could have a much shorter lifespan.	- Usability of the product. - The production method requires additives that might migrate (e.g. to the food). - Some plastics emit hazardous VOCs during their sourcing, but current alternatives without hazardous VOCs could have a much shorter lifespan. - To use fewer materials in the product itself, additional products will be needed to support use		- Preferred end-of-use scenario limits the use of combined materials with optimal properties.

		(e.g. potentially hazardous adhesives to install the product).		
End-of-Use	- Selected polymers and their required additives might limit the end-of-use options.	- Optimising manufacturing processes may reduce end-of-use options.	- Non-negotiable design requirements (e.g. barrier properties, installation or function of the product) lead to materials/ contaminations during the use phase with low(er) recycling potential.	

Note that data gaps are encountered at every phase of the life cycle. One of these data gaps is the lack of (comparable) emissions data throughout the supply chain. Design teams should not neglect data gaps and should not assume there are no sustainability implications. They should strive to fill these in wherever possible, especially for life cycle phases where damage to human health and ecosystems is to be expected based on available benchmarks. The teams should explicitly keep track of unknowns along the way. When an appropriate disclosure is missing, a sensitivity analysis (to see how important an environmental release might be), exposure testing or substitution for safer chemicals is advised.

There can also be significant variation in emissions between manufacturing facilities for the same base polymer material. The theoretical embodiment of the product concept should be put to the test with practical knowledge from specific suppliers who will provide the material and relevant circular processors who will most likely treat the products at their end-of-use. The sustainable design goals, life cycle considerations and trade-offs help guide the discussions with these stakeholders.

8.2. Dealing with Trade-Offs

In the case of trade-offs, designers and engineers will have to carefully evaluate considerations to favour one over the other. This process is guided by the ranking of the sustainable design goals and the non-negotiable conditions defined in Chapter 3. Transparency throughout this process is important to support credibility and ensure that decisions are traceable.

To illustrate how to deal with trade-offs, the example in Chapter 3, where closing resource loops is prioritised over slowing and narrowing resource loops for prioritising design goals (see Figure 3.1), is used to examine three trade-offs in the case of detergent bottles (Figure 8.1). The ranking example was as follows: 1. Select materials with inherently low risk/hazard; 2a. Use secondary feedstock or biobased feedstock, 2b. Have a commercial 'afterlife' (recycling); 3. Generate no waste; 4. Have a commercial 'afterlife' (other aspects).

The underlined terms in Figure 8.1 are decisive in the reasoning. The circled trade-offs are the ones that have been prioritised based on the reasoning in the right column. This approach can also be adopted to deal with the trade-offs emerging within the life cycle phases.

Figure 8.1. Example of trade-offs (two left columns) and how to deal with them (right column)

Trade-offs (examples)			Reasoning (examples)
Preserve natural capital	vs	Use commercial circular end-of-use paths	According to the ranking, avoiding damages to human health and ecosystems is more important than incorporating recycled plastic. A Life Cycle Assessment (LCA) of the concept showed that the impact of reducing transport was higher than that of using recycled plastic.
Highly concentrated detergent leads to fewer transport movements but requires bottle with premium chemical resistance unavailable from recycled feedstock.	or	Using recycled feedstock for bottling less concentrated detergent requiring more transport movements.	
Product marketing	vs	Use commercial circular end-of-use paths & preserve natural capital	Marketing is part of the negotiable design requirements (i.e., wants). According to the ranking, sustainability and circularity thus have to be prioritised.
Bottles made from virgin feedstock allow for transparent or bright coloured bottles.	or	Bottles made from secondary feedstock allow for less bright colours (rHDPE) and might have a grey/yellow discolouration for transparent rPET bottles but reduce the environmental footprint.	
Cost reduction	vs	Close material loops	
Low prices of virgin PET with premium aesthetics.	or	High prices for recycled feedstock with slightly reduced aesthetics.	A non-negotiable maximum price was fixed in the design brief. To close resource loops as much as possible, as much recycled content will be integrated as the budget allows. Discussions with the makers of the design brief are encouraged to stimulate the selection of more sustainable plastic.

Chapter 9. Conclusions and Recommended Next Steps

This chapter presents the overall conclusions of the document and offers next steps that could be taken to improve sustainable design of plastics from a chemicals perspective. It also provides a case example of the approach described in the document.

9.1. Conclusions

This report examines the chemicals perspective of the material selection process to inform designers and engineers on how to manage the complexity of finding sustainable plastic for their products. The main contributions of this study are an overview of the main steps of this process, and a set of generalizable sustainable design goals, life cycle considerations, and trade-offs.

The main steps of the sustainable plastic selection from a chemicals perspective are summarised in Figure 9.1. The case of a detergent bottle is used to illustrate the steps with examples and is not meant to be prescriptive, nor capture all sources of information. In a real world scenario, all information available needs to be taken into account at each step in order to inform decision-making.

9.2. Limitations and Recommended Next Steps

Knowledge gaps. Note that scientific insights on chemicals are not always available, because not all chemicals in a finished plastic product have been identified, and because hazard data may not be available for all known chemicals. It is also complex and difficult to have a complete assessment of the chemicals in products. Make sure to report the process as transparently as possible to note what is known and where data gaps were encountered, and of what type the data gaps were (e.g. chemical information and toxicological data).

Ongoing chemistry discovery, new substances, and material availability. Note that chemistry is a continuum of discovery, with new materials being brought to the marketplace over time. Designers should be mindful of new materials able to create improved outcomes for products and their operating environment.

Integrate sustainability design goals earlier in the design process. In this study, the sustainable design goals are formulated in the second step of the sustainable plastic selection process. Implicitly, sustainability becomes less of a priority compared to the previous design requirements (e.g. mechanical and electrical properties). However, it is ideally taken into account earlier on in the design process. It was assumed that a Design for a circular economy approach was adopted, but sustainable design goals have to be an integral part of the design requirement stage of the design process (see Figure 1.2). As a result, ambitious innovations in system, service, product, and material design will be triggered earlier on.

Broaden the scope to include other material families. This study focused on sustainable plastics. However, plastic may not be the most sustainable family of materials for a specific (part of the) product to begin with. The chemical perspective could also consider, for instance, metals, ceramics, natural (wool and wood) or composite materials.

Involve more stakeholders. Designers and engineers were considered the main actors in selecting sustainable plastics. Nevertheless, in a circular economy, the whole value chain should be involved to implement more sustainable plastic solutions. Collaborations should be stimulated to foster innovations at a systems level. Also, designers and engineers often do not have full control over the design brief, meaning that decision makers should also be trained on the subject.

Figure 9.1. Main steps of the sustainable plastic selection process from a chemicals perspective and a case example

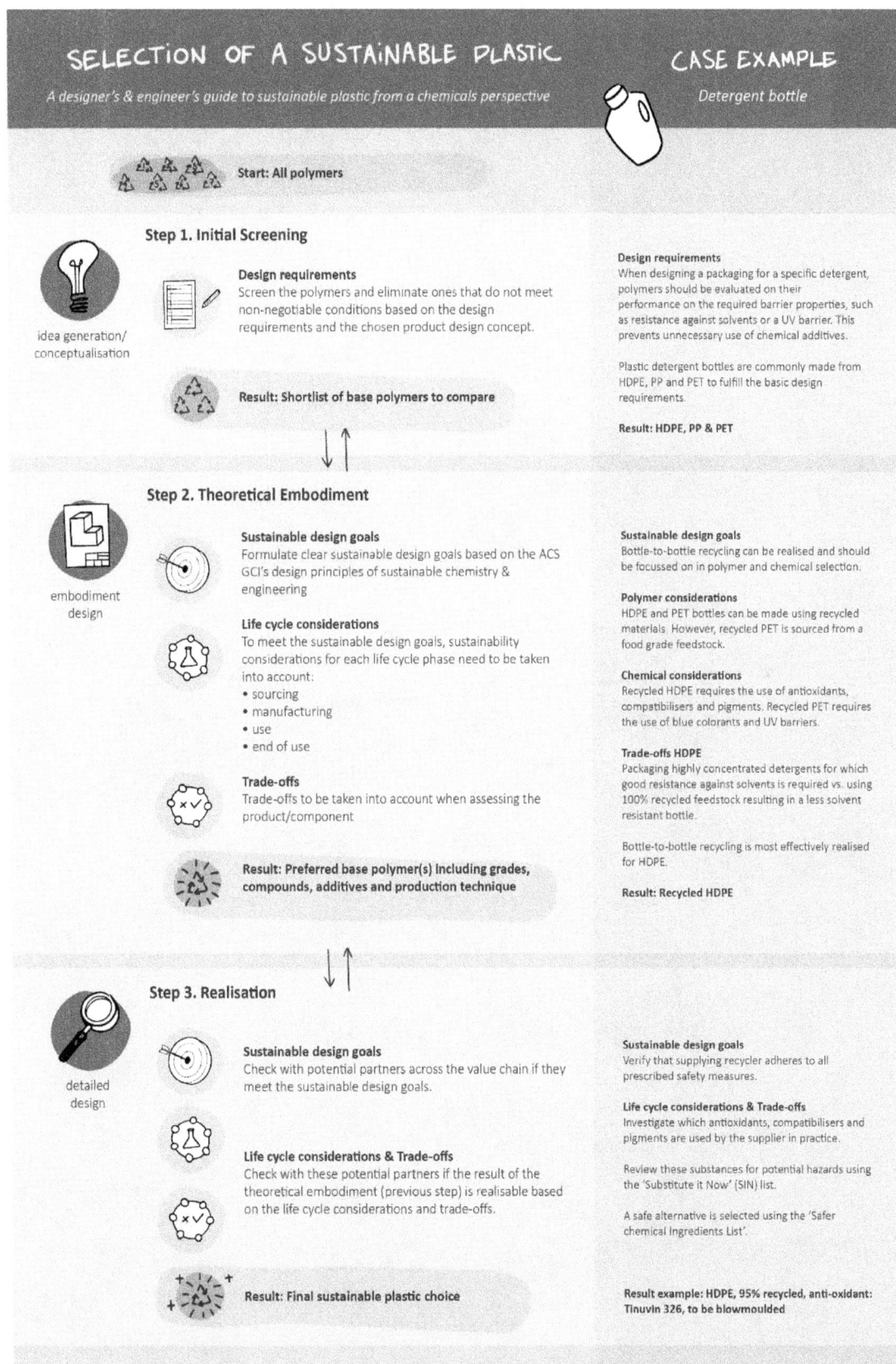

Annex A. Overview of Relevant Methods, Tools and Metrics

This is a non-exhaustive compilation of various methods, tools, and metrics specific to the chemicals perspective on sustainable plastics that could further help in the selection process. Further recommendations or guidance on the use of these tools is not within the scope of this report. These tools are listed here as examples and additional information on tools can also be found in Technical Tools and Approaches in the Design of Sustainable Plastics (OECD 2018b).

Measuring sustainability

Assessing Chemical Process Sustainability with Gauging Reaction Effectiveness for the Environmental Sustainability of Chemistries with a Multi-Objective Process Evaluator (GREENSCOPE) | US EPA – tool for the sustainability assessment of chemical processes

GaBi– Life cycle assessment (LCA) Software

LCIA: the ReCiPe model | RIVM - Methodology for the Impact Assessment in an LCA

SimaPro - LCA Software

The Economic Input-Output LCA tool | Carnegie Mellon University – Online tool to perform an Economic Input-Output LCA

Measuring circularity

Circle Scan | Circle Economy – Method to identify opportunities for companies, governments, and organisations to become more circular

Circular assessment | Circle Economy – Online tool to help businesses understand the different operational and organisational aspects of the Circular Economy

Circular IQ – Platform that helps optimise circularity of purchasing processes through data collection, reporting and analysis

Circular Transition Indicators Tool | WBCSD – Online software tool to measure a company's circular performance based on the Circular Transition Indicators

Circularity Calculator | IDEAL&CO – Tool to measure, communicate and improve the circularity of products.

Circularity check | Ecopreneur – Online tool determining the circularity of a product and/or service based on a questionnaire

Circulytics | Ellen MacArthur Foundation – Tool to measure circularity of companies

Cradle-to-Cradle certification – measure of safe and sustainable products based on the certification scheme of the Cradle to Cradle Products Innovation Institute

IMPACT (TNO) – Scientific method for establishing the circularity of products

Madaster Circularity indicator | Madaster & EPEA – Tool to determine the circularity of a building

Metabolism analysis | Metabolic – Method considering the material, energy, water and waste flows of cities, companies, and organisations.

Optimal SCANS – System for sustainable and circular purchasing and monitoring of organisations, products, and services

ReNtry | Rendemint – Part of the PRP circular E-procurement tool that ensures optimal preservation of resources

Recyclability assessment

APR Design ® Guide | The Association of Plastics Recyclers – guide for packaging designers to measure each aspect of a package design against recycling compatibility criteria per frequently used plastics

Design Guidelines | European PET Bottle Platform – General design guidelines for PET bottles

Recyclability By Design | RECOUP Recycling – Guidelines to help industry understand the full technicalities of plastic packaging recyclability.

RecyClass Tool | Plastics Recyclers Europe – Online tool that helps check the recyclability of packaging and gives advice on improvement

Chemical Hazard Assessment (CHA)

California Safe Consumer Products Alternatives Analysis Guide | Department of Toxic Substances Control – Comprehensive list of CHA methods and databases

CHA database | IC2 – Database to search for Greenscreen and Quick Chemical Assessment Tool assessments

Food Contact Chemicals database (FCCdb) | Food Packaging Forum - inventory on hazardous chemicals in plastic packaging with a priority list of chemicals to avoid

Groh, K. et al. (2020) "Overview of intentionally used food contact chemicals and their hazards." *Environment International,* Vol. 150.

Groh, K., et al. (2018). "Overview of known plastic packaging-associated chemicals and their hazards." *Science of The Total Environment,* Vol. 651, No. 2.

Globally Harmonised System (GHS) of Classification and Labelling of Chemicals United Nations Economic Commission for Europe (2021) (9th Revised Edition), New York and Geneva

GreenScreen® – Tool identifying hazardous chemicals and safer alternatives based on GHS and the US EPA Design for the Environment methods and including an overall chemical benchmark score

Plastics Scorecard Version 1.0 | BizNGO - scores polymeric materials by evaluating individual chemicals and aggregating their associated GreenScreen Benchmark scores

Quick Chemical Assessment Tool – developed by the Washington State Department of Ecology for small and medium enterprises with limited toxicological expertise and resources

Restricted Substances List | Cradle-to-Cradle Products Innovation Institute, - Restrictions to all products seeking Cradle to Cradle certification

Safer Chemical Ingredients List | US EPA – List of chemical ingredients organised by functional-use class based on the Safer Choice Program

Safer Choice Standard and Criteria | Safer Choice | US EPA – Standard that identifies the requirements that products and their ingredients must meet to earn the Safer Choice label

SIN list from ChemSec – List of chemicals identified for substitution based on their properties

Sustainable Futures | US EPA – Program that gives chemical developers the same risk-screening models that EPA uses

Toxicity Forecasting | US EPA - Toxicity Forecaster (ToxCast) includes data and predictive models on thousands of chemicals

Scivera Lens – Chemical Hazard Assessment tool with a system with 23 toxicological endpoints

Exposure Assessment

Exposure Map: Greggs, W. et al. (2019) "Qualitative Approach to Comparative Exposure in Alternatives Assessment", *Integrated Environmental Assessment and Management*, Vol.15, No.6.

Hierarchy of controls | NIOSH – Hierarchy of methods to control exposures to occupational hazards

Rapid Chemical Exposure and Dose Research | US EPA – Tools, models, databases, and other resources to estimate exposure for thousands of chemicals

Total Exposure Assessment Methodology (TEAM) | US EPA – Study that measured exposure to Volatile Organic Compounds in the air, drinking water and exhaled breath

Alternatives assessment

Design for the Environment Alternatives Assessments | Safer Choice | US EPA – Assessment that characterises chemical hazards based on a full range of human health and environmental information.

Online training on analysis of alternatives | ECHA – Introductory online training on analysis of alternatives to hazardous substances

Substitution and alternatives assessment tool selector | OECD – Tool selector provides information on online resources and software that can be used in conducting chemical substitutions or alternatives assessments

Databases, Life Cycle Inventory (LCI) datasets and Environmental Product Declarations (EPD)

CompTox Chemistry Dashboard | US EPA – Database of chemicals

CPCat Database | US EPA - Chemical and Product Database categorizing chemicals to usage or function

eChemPortal | OECD – Global Portal to Information on Chemical Substances

Eco-profiles | Plastics Europe – LCI datasets and Environmental Product Declarations (EPD) for plastics

EcoInvent database – LCI dataset

ECOTOXicology knowledgebase | US EPA – publicly available knowledgebase with toxicity data on aquatic life, terrestrial plants and wildlife

Information on Chemicals | ECHA– Source of information on the chemicals manufactured and imported in Europe

PubChem Compound database | US NLM - Database of chemicals

QSAR toolbox | OECD – Software application intended to fill gaps in (eco)toxicity data to assess the hazards of chemicals

Regulatory check

EUCLEF tool | ECHA - explains duties linked to chemicals under various pieces of EU legislation.

References

OECD (2018b), "Technical Tools and Approaches in the Design of Sustainable Plastics: Background paper 2. OECD Global Forum on Environment: Plastics in a Circular Economy", *Series on Risk Management*, No. 52, OECD, Paris, https://www.oecd.org/chemicalsafety/risk-management/technical-tools-and-approaches-in-the-design-of-sustainable-plastics.pdf

About the OECD Chemical Safety and Biosafety Programme

The Environment, Health and Safety Division publishes free-of-charge documents in twelve different series: Testing and Assessment; Good Laboratory Practice and Compliance Monitoring; Pesticides; Biocides; Risk Management; Harmonisation of Regulatory Oversight in Biotechnology; Safety of Novel Foods and Feeds; Chemical Accidents; Pollutant Release and Transfer Registers; Emission Scenario Documents; Safety of Manufactured Nanomaterials; and Adverse Outcome Pathways. More information about the Environment, Health and Safety Programme and EHS publications is available on the OECD's World Wide Web site (www.oecd.org/chemicalsafety/). More publications in the Series on Risk Management are available at https://www.oecd.org/chemicalsafety/risk-management.

The Inter-Organisation Programme for the Sound Management of Chemicals (IOMC)

This publication was developed in the IOMC context. The contents do not necessarily reflect the views or stated policies of individual IOMC Participating Organisations.

The Inter-Organisation Programme for the Sound Management of Chemicals (IOMC) was established in 1995 following recommendations made by the 1992 UN Conference on Environment and Development to strengthen co-operation and increase international co-ordination in the field of chemical safety. The Participating Organisations are FAO, ILO, UNDP, UNEP, UNIDO, UNITAR, WHO, World Bank and OECD. The purpose of the IOMC is to promote co-ordination of the policies and activities pursued by the Participating Organisations, jointly or separately, to achieve the sound management of chemicals in relation to human health and the environment.

IOMC

INTER-ORGANIZATION PROGRAMME FOR THE SOUND MANAGEMENT OF CHEMICALS

A cooperative agreement among **FAO, ILO, UNDP, UNEP, UNIDO, UNITAR, WHO, World Bank and OECD**

www.ingramcontent.com/pod-product-compliance
Lightning Source LLC
Chambersburg PA
CBHW081512200326
41518CB00015B/2478